refuge in

things small

by Mike Travisano

For permission requests,
contact info@refugeinsmallthings.com.

ISBN 979-8-9890664-0-7
Printed in the United States of America
Independently published
Edited by Taylor Plimpton
Cover, typeset, and illustration by Jess Gibson

108 Entries

Table of Contents

000 Preface

Reading the word 'preface,'
I know that I'm reading the word 'preface.'

Breathing in,
I know that I'm
breathing in.

Breathing out,
I know that I'm
breathing out.

Turning the page,
I know that I'm turning the page.

The Prison Is Locked from the Inside

I can be free from suffering and the causes of suffering.
I can be free from thinking that my life is not my own.
I can be free from emotions that carry me to places
I would never choose.
I can be free from handing control of my state of being
to things outside of myself.
I can be free from a life ruled by the things I own.
I can be free from the thought that I am only as valuable
as what I do for money.
I can be free from the belief that I'm not enough.
I can be free from what I did or did not do,
from what I should or should not do, and
from what I can or cannot do.
I can be free from what happened.
I can be free from the thought that I am alone and temporary.

I can be free to experience joy.
I can be free to love myself and others unconditionally,
no matter what lives in the corners of my mind's basement.
I can be free to grieve when that is what life asks of me.
I can be free to forgive (and to be forgiven).
I can be free to try (and to fail).
I can be free to accept the kindness, love, and compassion
of others (and to offer it as well).
I can be free to express what I feel in my heart
by the way I live.
I can be free to let go.
I can be free to choose my own thoughts.
I can be free to create my own experience of the world.

I can be free.

The Practice of Enlightenment

Master, how long will it take until I attain true enlightenment?

A lifetime.

A lifetime?
What if I were to practice for eighteen hours each day, seven days per week without fail. How long will it take then?

Every day without fail?

Yes.

For eighteen hours each day?

Yes, eighteen hours every day!

And without missing even one single day?

Yes, without ever missing one day!

500 lifetimes.

Enlightenment is not a one-time event. It isn't something attained or achieved, like the flicking of a spiritual light switch.

It's reminding myself of what I already know
to be true in my heart.
It's the everyday, moment-to-moment mindful
act of being.
It's ongoing intent and discipline.
It's the willingness to overcome the tremendous
barrier of what I think I already know.
It's throwing the illusory goal of perfection
out of every possible window.

It's noticing what is right in front of me.
It's growing in tiny, tiny ways.
It's befriending the darkest places within myself
and others with compassion.

Enlightenment isn't magic, and it's not reserved for some
small, deserved few. Enlightenment is open to everyone
everywhere and depends on nothing but the desire to take
one step, no matter how small, and then to take another.

003 A Lamp Unto Myself

As the Buddha lay dying, his close friend, Ananda,
was despondent. He wondered how the community could
go on without him. He wondered how he could go on without
him. He was scared for himself, and for the people he loved.
He asked the Buddha what they should do, and
the Buddha replied:

> Be lamps unto yourselves.
> Rely on yourselves.
> Hold fast to the truth as a lamp.
> Seek salvation alone in this.

A short while later, the Buddha spoke his final words:

> All things pass.
> All things break down.
> Work tirelessly to find what is true.

Someday, maybe even today, the only thing standing between
me and some bottomless black plummet is going to be what
I know to be true in my own heart.

When that day comes,

> I may be terrified. I may panic.
> I may flail around and claw the air for help like
> I'm drowning.

I don't rule these possibilities out, and I hope I'm never so arrogant as to assume that I'd do otherwise, but until then—

I'm going to work hard to find answers.
I'm going to ask questions until I'm sure
that I understand.
I'm going to accept nothing as true unless
it is as clear and as real to me as a jewel resting
in the palm of my own hand.

I'm going to be my own lamp.

004 Mindfulness 101

I am who I think I am.

As I grew up, I learned what to believe and how to think:

> who and what to like or dislike, which groups
> to be a part of or avoid, and what a good life
> should look like.

I was further shaped by my life's tectonics:

> the spiritual overhaul of true love and the gift
> of a wonderful child, the shocking surprise
> of aging, and the gaping maw of death.

I carry around who I think I am like a big briefcase of stories
about how the world works, which:

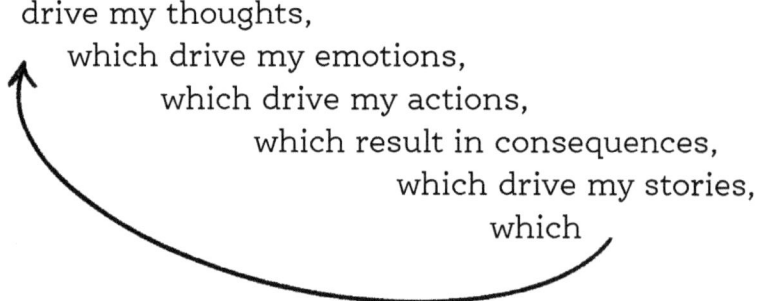

drive my thoughts,
  which drive my emotions,
    which drive my actions,
      which result in consequences,
        which drive my stories,
          which

But what if the story I'm telling myself isn't true?
What if it's causing suffering for myself or others or both?
What if it's doing harm to myself or others or both?

As I develop the skill of mindfulness, I learn to notice
the emotions that cause me to suffer—as though I'm hearing
the ringing of a bell (or maybe an air raid siren).

I learn to identify the thoughts that cause those emotions, I learn to understand the story behind those thoughts, and if my story isn't clear or helpful, I learn to choose a different story.

I am who I think I am. I create my own experience of the world, and I have the power to change it if I so choose.

Me as a Matter of Perspective

I am MUCH MORE THAN who I TEND TO think I am.

I tend to think I'm some "something" that lives somewhere behind my eyeballs, drives my bag of meat and bones around, and tries not to bump into stuff. I win sometimes and I also don't. I sometimes feel OK, but I often don't. I often feel small. I often feel temporary. I often feel alone.

If I look again, though, the lines between "me" and "not me" start to get blurry:

> I breathe air, and without it, there would
> be no "me."
>> (Am I the air?)
> I eat food, and without it, there would
> be no "me."
>> (Am I what I eat?)
> I stand on the ground, and without it, there
> would be no "me."
>> (Am I the ground?)
> I interact, learn, grow, and change, and without
> those, there would be no "me."
>> (Am I my interactions, lessons, growth, and change?)
> I have parents, who had parents, who had parents
> (ad infinitum), and without them, there would
> be no "me."
>> (Am I my parents, my parents' parents,
>> my parents' parents' parents, ad infinitum?)

Nothing exists in and of itself.
Everything that seems separate is really made from
connections that depend on each other. Everything
is a relationship, including me. This is my True Self.
This is me as the connection with all things.
This is Oneness.

But I am still "me."
I'm a person and I experience the world. I love pizza and horror movies and heavy metal. This is my ever-evolving Ego Self. This is my humanity.

My True Self and my Ego Self aren't two separate selves, they're just ways to describe aspects of who I am, depending on how I choose to look at it.

There is no need to transcend, starve, or "kill" my Ego Self, as it's through my Ego Self that I awaken to my True Self, just as it's through the realization of my True Self that I learn to love and care for my Ego Self. They work together like two hands on a guitar: one frets, the other plucks the strings— and together they are music.

The Tree

If I think of the universe and everything in it as "The Great Tree of All Things," then I tend to think of myself as

a tiny little weird fruit

that grows on a tiny little weird branch

far, far away from the trunk.

From way out here,
I see myself
only as that
one little fruit,
spending all my time
looking at the other fruit,
wishing I was juicier
and prettier,
and in doing so,
forgetting that

I'm connected to a branch

that's connected to the trunk

that connects to all the other branches,

leaves, fruit, ground,
and sky.

In my forgetting, I forget that
there's a tree at all.

More than that, I forget that

I AM THE TREE

just as much as I am

the tiny little weird fruit

that grows from it.

While the fruit was born,

will grow, will ripen in the sun,

will be munched on by bugs,

will be jostled in the wind,

and will inevitably

wither and fall,

THE TREE
is more than these things—
beyond the fruit's pain,
beyond its smallness,
beyond its birth,
and beyond
its death.

007 refuge in small things

I think of a time when I felt truly alive.
I think of when I've laughed so hard that my face hurt
and I couldn't breathe.
I think of the smell of my dogs' warm fur as they're sleeping.
I think of big bear hugs with my best friends.
I think of someone who holds my heart.
I think of celebrating their happiness and being so joyful
that I can't speak.
I think of sitting quietly and fully with them in true sadness
or grief.

I know that these experiences aren't powerful by mistake—
they're our birthright: 13.8 billion years of change and
chance arriving here at this very moment, floating on a rock
in the vastness of space and getting to feel my chest well
with the incandescence of joy, wonder, awe, and love.

No job or lack of one could improve the sun rising over
the ocean.
No accomplishment or failure could change the leaves
dancing in the breeze.
No title earned or stripped could dim the shine of the moon.
No amount of money gained or lost could change how
the wind feels on my face.
No past deep suffering or future fear could change my love
for those who live in my heart.

I take refuge in these "tiny," "mundane," and
"inconsequential" things, and I'm reminded of the miracle
that there is anything at all. I'm reminded, in this great and
mysterious something,

> That nothing is inconsequential.
> That I am not inconsequential.
> That I am here.
> That I get to notice.

Each night, I remind myself of this like a prayer:

I take refuge in small things, like my tiny dog
sleeping in the patch of sunshine coming
through the window,
the smell of the pizza in the back of the car
as I drive home,
that little kid in the parking lot's silly little laugh,
the moon behind those fast-moving purple clouds.

Kanzeon

There is an innate goodness in the world.
I know this is true because I have experienced it.

I have experienced others patiently not giving up on me,
long after I had.

I have experienced friends and strangers going out of their
way to help me for no discernible reason and without
expectation of anything in return.

I have experienced others carrying the weight of my burdens
time and time again, because they wouldn't allow me to bear
them alone.

I have hidden myself away in despair, only to be found and
rescued by the insistent weight of a paw on my leg and
a soft, furry head on my lap.

I have been utterly lost, only to find unexpected paths where
I never thought to look.

I have met the Bodhisattva of Compassion,
In some places called Kanzeon.
In others, Quan-Yin.
In others, Avalokiteshvara.

I have witnessed their 10,000 arms reaching out to those
in need, myself included. I have chanted the spell
of their mantra:

    Kanji Zai Bosa
    Kanji Zai Bosa
    Kanji Zai Bosa

And I've heard their reply.

Each night, I offer this prayer:

I take refuge in having asked for help and
having received it.
I am thankful for the compassion, support, and
help I've been given,
May I return it as best as I can.
May I be helpful.
May I not take the grace of others and
the goodness in front of me for granted.

009 The Vast Net of Indra

See in the site of the Buddha's enlightenment
Lotuses and Jewel Nets, all pure;
Flames of light in whirls appear from here,
Music of bells and chimes comes from the clouds.
—From the Flower-Garland Sutra (Avatamsaka)

———————————————

I am the infinite web of interdependent connections, both intentional and unintentional, both beautiful and tragic.

I am the vast Net of Indra, with perfectly clear jewels at each knot, reflecting all the others in their facets.

I am every decision I've ever made. I bow to both the unfortunate ones and the fortunate. I bow to the simple and the profound, knowing that each brought me to everything for which I am most grateful today.

I am the spinach I ate for lunch, just as I am also the truck and driver who delivered it from its farm, the farmer who planted it, the rain that watered it, and the sunlight that fed it. I bow to them all, knowing that without any one of them, there would be no spinach, there would be no lunch, and there would be no me.

I am everyone who came before me, knowing that they blazed the path that created my own. I honor it and pray that my own path leads to a better future for everyone after me, knowing that I am their path, too.

I am every event, both the worldly and the galactic, the horrific and the beautiful. I am the product of their response, and in turn, I respond.

I bow to being both the One thing and the individual expression of it. May the quality of my being inspire my actions to end suffering for all beings everywhere and everywhen.

Each night, I offer this prayer:

> I take refuge in not knowing where and when I begin, and where and when I end.
>
> I take refuge in knowing
> that I am not separate,
> that I am whole,
> that I am complete.

010 Feeding the Hungry Ghosts

I see you, Hungry Ghosts. I know you're there. I see your
mouths stretched wide, your impossibly thin necks, and
your horribly distended stomachs. I know that no matter
how much I feed you, you'll demand more. I know that
you're starving. I know this is why you haunt me.

> I see you as I watch TV, but can't pay attention.
> I see you at the foot of my bed, keeping me
> from sleep.
> I see you on a perfect sunny day when I'm
> convinced that I have no right to it.
> I see you in my jealousy and anger.
> I see you in my unworthiness.
> I see you in my regret.
> I see you when I think my life would be better
> if I was someone, anyone other than who I am.

I see you, but I don't look away and I don't run.
I welcome you to sit with me and share a meal.

I feed you the wisdom that while I experience delusion, hatred,
and greed, I am not my delusion, hatred, and greed. I am not
my sense of lack or suffering.

I feed you the wisdom that I've succumbed to my thoughts
of "not enough" before. I've succeeded in attaining what
I thought would fix me, only to find the delusion of "not
enough" return again and again.

I feed you the wisdom that in my True Self I am whole, that
there is nothing missing, nothing more required.

I feed you compassion and kindness. With my arm around
you like a true friend, I say,

How awful it must be to feel like you do,
to forever crave what will never truly help you.
I see you behind the hurtful actions of others,
knowing in this way that they suffer just as I do,
that we are the same.

Be at peace, Hungry Ghosts. No matter how frightening you
appear, I see each and every one of you and meet you
as a friend.

Each night, I offer this prayer:

I take refuge in knowing that my Hungry Ghosts,
born from delusion, hatred, and greed, are not
who I really am, and not who others really are.
May they be fed with wisdom and compassion.
May they be at peace.

The Supreme Meal

Wondering what to make for dinner?

This recipe is the only one you'll ever need! Kids, adults, and the whole family just LOVE the Supreme Meal! Made with locally sourced fresh ingredients, this recipe for a LIFE LIVED FULLY requires zero effort but delivers BIG on flavor!

★★★★★ 1 review   Q 1 comment

Prep Time	**Cook Time**	**Serves**
0 minutes	0 minutes	All beings across space and time.

Ingredients:
1 exactly what you already have.
1 exactly who you already are.

Directions:
1. Mix 1 of exactly what you already have with 1 of exactly who you already are.
2. Awaken to the reality that all things are connected and depend on each other.
3. Live from this experience.

Reviews:

 ★★★★★
this_is_my_prayer_108:

I take refuge in knowing that
all the ingredients I need for a life lived fully
are exactly what I already have, and exactly
who I already am.

Love as a Round Trip

I search my heart for what I need most—for where I think
I fall short within myself—and I wish for it:

> May I feel connected and grateful and joyful
> and whole.

I choose someone I love, someone my heart naturally opens
to. I let my chest fill with the love I have for them, and on the
string that connects our hearts, I send my wish to them:

> May that wonderful being whom I love so very
> much feel connected and grateful and joyful
> and whole.

I move one circle out to a friend from work, an acquaintance,
or a colleague, and make the wish for them. I do it with such
intent that I'm sure they must feel it happen as I do:

> May that dude with the moustache in accounting
> feel connected and grateful and joyful and whole.

Expanding outward still, I search for someone I don't know
at all—the checkout person at the supermarket, the woman
in the car next to mine at the traffic light this morning, or the
guy I noticed mowing his lawn on my drive home. I open
my heart and send my wish:

> May that person who was ahead of me in line feel
> connected and grateful and joyful and whole.

Now, with all of the love I have within me, I call to mind
someone who bothers me—someone who frustrates
or angers me. This person truly challenges me, but I know
that poor behavior is just a symptom of suffering, and that
maybe if they had some of this wish, they'd feel better and
maybe not cause so much trouble around them:

> May that annoying grumpy jerk who I usually wish would just go jump in a lake feel connected and grateful and joyful and whole.

At this point, I imagine that I am my wish incarnate. I imagine I've channeled so much wonderful energy that supernovae may be jealous. I take a breath or two, and then I let it all go. I send it all out at once to everyone everywhere: to every kitten, every child and child soldier, every Wall Street banker and soup kitchen customer, every bird and bug, every fish, every tree:

> May all beings everywhere feel connected and grateful and joyful and whole.

But love is not one-way, it's a round trip, so I begin my journey home:

> With each following breath, I make the wish again for the one who troubles me, then for the person I don't know, then for my acquaintance, and once more for the ones I love the most.

I feel the connections again as I'm headed back to myself. The journey has been truly epic—I've visited (quite literally) everyone everywhere, and now I'm ready to channel all of that wonderful flow squarely back at myself once more:

> May I feel connected and grateful and joyful and whole.

Finally, I think of those who are lost in their suffering, still unable to make any wish for themselves, and I pray that they don't worry, because I've got them. They're in every wish that I make, every time:

May they feel the wave wash over them
any moment now.

Here it comes.

One Day

One day, I'm eating a banana in the kitchen and a work email pops up from the freaking ceo who asks me if i can put together the detail to walk the 37 million back to the 25 million and hell no i don't have that detail! it is all made up and not by me and where the hell are the higher up people who are involved with that? why aren't they jumping in? they're hiding, that's where, fucking cowards. and i love that he sends it on sunday morning. the sunday morning before my week off, no less. so i guess i get to hold the bag and make something up and look like an idiot to that condescending piece of shit and not to mention that i have to run to the store and the lawn needs to be mowed and now i have to do some work bullshit that i don't even understand and

and then it dawns on me that

I'm eating a banana in the kitchen. That's what's happening. That's what's really happening. There's a bird singing some kind of chant and the light is coming in so beautifully. There's an aliveness within me that I can feel, and I am thankful for all there is. I am thankful for this one day.

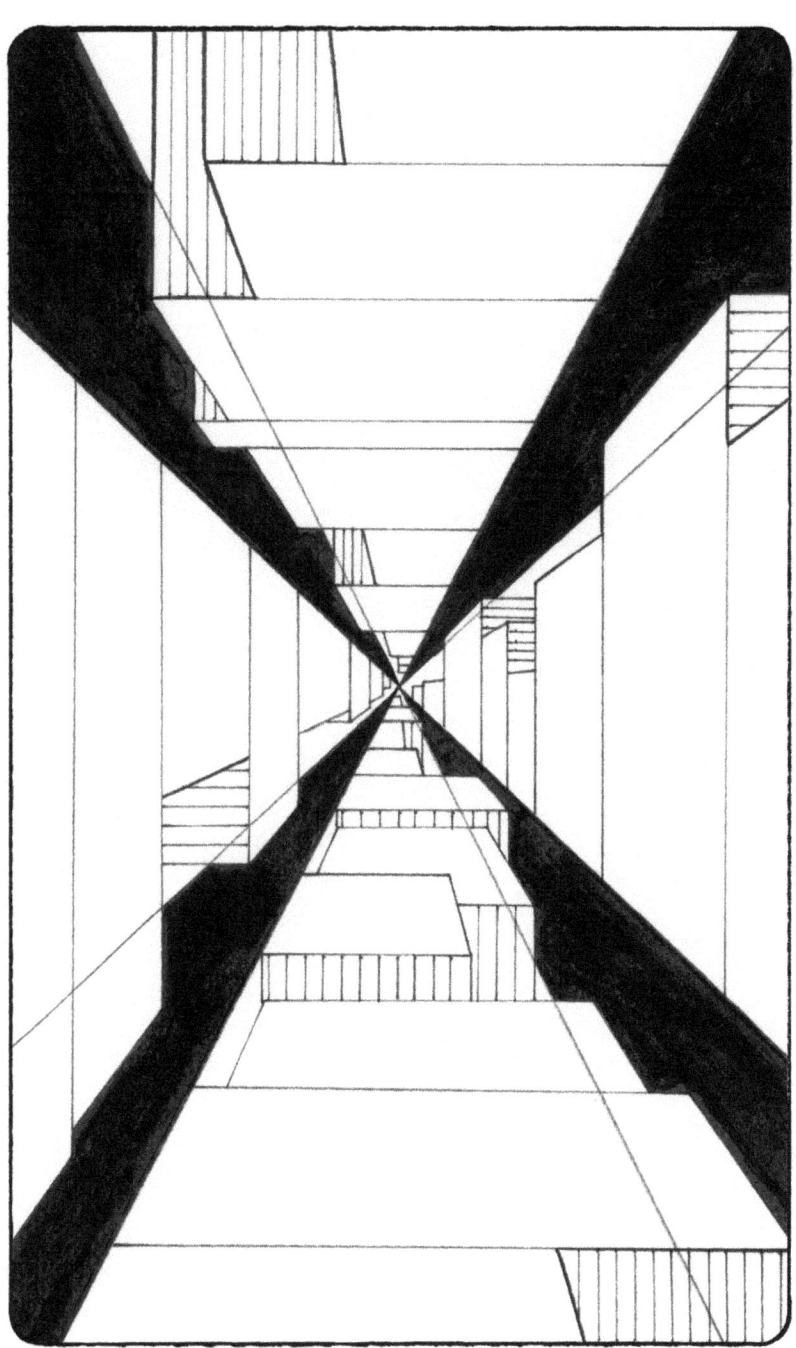

For many years,
I chased happiness.
Blame it on my culture or
my upbringing, or whatever,
but I thought that if I could
just do the right things and
acquire the right stuff and
be with the right people
(and stay away from the
wrong stuff and people), that
happiness would inevitably
come, and so I chased it
and did my very best to
disregard any notion that
there might be more than
just the chase.

But in truth,
I wasn't happy.
I just knew
in my heart that something
was missing.

Despite everything I had,
all of the things
and experiences,
I just couldn't shake
the feeling that no matter
what I did or had, that

I wasn't doing
what I should be doing,
I didn't have what
I should have,
I wasn't the person
I should be.

For nearly thirty years,
Siddhartha lived in absolute
comfort. His father, the great
King Suddhodana made
sure of it, insisting that the
young prince be provided
every luxury and pleasure
imaginable, so that he would
never experience hardship or
suffering, or anything that
might distract him from his
rightful place on the throne
or drive him to the outrageous
prophesy that he might
one day become a great
spiritual teacher.

But in truth,
Siddhartha wasn't happy,
and he knew
in his heart that something
was missing.

Despite all that he had,
every possible possession
and experience imaginable,
he couldn't stop
the voice within him
telling him that

he was not doing
what he should be doing,
he didn't have what
he thought he should have,
he wasn't the person
he believed he should be.

So I kept searching,
and wanting,
and craving the thing that
could finally deliver me
to the life of lightness and
ease that I knew must be out
there somewhere.

One night, at the risk
of sounding overly dramatic,
I had what one might call
"a dark night of the soul."
I couldn't sleep and
I couldn't stop my spiraling
thoughts, and all I wanted
to do was run away from
my life. It's like I came face
to face with the reality that
if I didn't make some sort
of change, someday I'd just
get sick, old, and die, and
wouldn't have experienced
the life I just know must be
out there. It was like a voice
within me was telling me to
run, to find my path,
to escape!

And so I did it. I quit
the life that was all I had
ever known. I followed
my passion and listened
to my heart. I quit my job
and began a search to find
a path out of suffering.

So he kept searching,
and wanting,
and craving the thing that
could finally deliver him
to the life of lightness and
ease that he knew must be out
there somewhere.

One night, restless and
wanting, Siddhartha escaped
from the palace and found
himself face to face with a
reality he could not have
imagined. As he rode through
the city with his friend and
chariot driver, Channa, he saw
for the first time in his life:
a sick person, an elderly
person, and a corpse on its
way to its pyre. Having been
sheltered from these his entire
life, the shock was profound,
but then Siddhartha witnessed
a fourth sight: a wandering
mendicant, a person dedicated
to finding a pathway out
of suffering.

And so Siddhartha renounced
his princely title and life
as the heir to the throne and
wandered the forests for seven
years, meditating, learning,
and searching for
a path out of suffering.

I plunged myself into my search, giving myself completely over to the idea that I could find happiness from my own doing. I read books and took classes. I learned to meditate, and I studied with "gurus," and much to my absolute amazement, I came to the most astonishing realization: Despite everything I had done and changed,

Driven to find an answer, Siddhartha explored ever more advanced teachers and drastic practices: meditating for countless hours, denying himself sleep, and going for prolonged periods without eating even a single grain of rice, and much to his absolute amazement, Siddhartha came to the most astonishing realization: Despite everything he had done and changed,

I still wasn't doing what I thought I should be doing. I still didn't have what I thought I should have. I still wasn't the person I believed I should be.

He still wasn't doing what he thought he should be doing. He still didn't have what he thought he should have. He still wasn't the person he believed he should be.

And once the bewilderment and confusion passed, it dawned on me that I was no better off than when I began. I wasn't happy in my "first life," and I still wasn't happy in my second!

Siddhartha rested, recovered, and reflected. He realized deeply that, despite all that he had done and changed, he was no closer to finding an end to suffering as an ascetic than he was as a prince.

I couldn't help but wonder: If I couldn't be happy in the "rat race," and I also couldn't be happy out of it, could happiness be found somewhere else?

He wondered: If happiness wasn't to be found in riches, and it wasn't to be found in denying them, then could it be found in some other way?

Could there possibly be
something "in between"
the two; something
"in the middle,"
somehow?

Could it be possible that it
isn't what I do or have
that is the source of
my own happiness, peace,
and contentment,
but

Could there possibly be
something "in between"
them: something not found in
one extreme or the other, but
in the middle, somehow?

Could it be possible that it
isn't what we do or have
that is the source of
our own happiness, peace,
and contentment,
but

some
thing
else
?

The Great Battle

As Siddhartha sat under the common fig that would one day be called the Bodhi tree, the great fiend within Siddhartha's mind, Mara, the Lord of Desires, gnashed his teeth and fangs: "Who is this thing to challenge me? Who dares to lay claim to the Throne of Enlightenment?"

Disgusted and incensed, Mara drew forth his vast army from the darkest depths of Siddhartha's consciousness, summoning his sons, Confusion, Indulgence, and Pride, as well as his daughters, Lust, Delight, and Craving. He called forth his legions of demons, their mouths yawning with savage teeth and wagging tongues, their shrieking, baying, and howling consuming the earth and heavens, their rolling, wild eyes, burning like disks of fire.

Siddhartha did not stir. In stillness, he saw the terrible demon within himself, and he donned the armor of Virtue, adorned with the jewels of Patience, Generosity, Energy, and Concentration, and with a breath, strung his great bow of Compassion and nocked the arrow of Wisdom.

With a roar, Mara's armies set loose arrows of their own, sending a great volley of Hatred, Greed, and Ignorance, only to watch as each one floated harmlessly to the ground, turned to flowers in the peaceful clarity of Siddhartha's mind.

The demon heaved the spears of Infatuation and Jealousy, but Siddhartha's Generous Heart became like the great king of the eagles, the Garuda, who effortlessly plucked each one from the air.

With quivering hate, Mara sent forth the venomous snakes of Anger and Loathing, but Siddhartha recognized them as merely suffering in disguise, and compassionately turned each into soft red lotus petals.

The great fiend charged his giant war elephant of Pride, Girimekhala, but Siddhartha's Humility became a lion whose gaze alone sent the trumpeting beast from the field.

The demon blew the vast Wind of Lies, but Siddhartha was protected by the Mountain of Truth, which no wind can surmount.

Enraged, desperate, and wild, Mara spat, "Who are you to claim the throne of Nirvana and end all suffering? What right do you have, you worthless, putrid, nothing human? You are alone! You are small, insignificant, powerless, and weak! Who would ever deign speak for you!"

Siddhartha softly touched the ground in front of him. The air quickened, the grasses danced, the waters bent, and the whole world shook as Vasundhara, the Goddess of the Earth, emerged from behind him, towering far into the sky. "I speak for him. I bear him witness," and with both hands, wrung a torrent of water from her hair, an ocean born from the karma of Siddhartha's words and deeds.

With terror and panic in their eyes, the demon king and his vast army were washed away in the flood, utterly defeated.

The one who was once called Siddhartha opened his eyes and saw Venus shining brightly in the morning sky. Now the Tathagata—the awakened "gone thus forth"—he smiled and uttered, "How wonderful! This awakening is within us all. We are awakened together."

The sky grew clear and gleaming, and a shower of flower blossoms fell upon the earth.

The First Truth is that life includes suffering.
For all the wonder and magic and good times and rainbows,
life can feel really shitty sometimes. Sure, there are some
good things, like vacations and (most) Saturdays, but
I always have this low-level hum in my chest or gut. I feel
inadequate. I feel guilty. I feel stressed. I feel totally alone.
I'm terrified. I'm worthless. I'm full of rage and hatred and
I don't care. I'm depressed and utterly despairing. Sometimes
I don't want to be here. Sometimes I wish I never was.

**The Second Truth is that I suffer because I crave
things and experiences that I think will fix me.**
I have a picture in my mind of what life should look like
and I can't stop thinking that if only __ would happen, then
I'd be OK: If only they'd be different. If only I wouldn't have
said that. If only they'd go away. If only they'd stay. If only
I wasn't so fat so thin so bald so tall so lazy so nervous so
weird so gay so old so worthless so poor so pale so uncool
so needy so emotional so so so so so so so

**The Third Truth is that if I get what I crave,
it won't stop my suffering—only stopping the
craving will.**
That gap that I think exists between who I think I should
be and who I think I am is not true or clear. I know if I had
any of the things that I think would fix me, I'd only want
something else. I know it because I've done it before! I've
gotten what I thought I needed, only to end up wanting
something else later.

The Fourth Truth is "The Noble Eightfold Path."
Instead of focusing on not craving (which would be like not
picturing an elephant), I choose to live in a new and different
way. I choose to live with purpose across eight aspects
in which I experience the world, forever discovering
and refining:

1. My view:
How I understand myself, the world, and each thing and being in it.

2. My intent:
How I approach each challenge, each day, each moment.

3. How I speak:
Recognizing that how I communicate with others matters and has an impact, I'll do my best to be honest and to not be divisive or abusive.

4. How I act:
I'll recognize that I am the heir of my own actions. I will do no harm. I won't take what isn't mine. I'll treat my relationships as sacred and precious.

5. My livelihood:
I'll come to know that how I am in my work matters at least as much as what I do.

6. The effort of my practice:
I'll make how I am an ongoing diligent act.

7. How well I am able to concentrate:
I'll work to develop the skill to focus my own mind on what I choose.

8. How mindful I am:
I'll continue to explore the quality of the stories I tell myself, ensuring that my thoughts and beliefs are clear.

As I walk this Eightfold Path, I cultivate a life of my own choosing. I allow the artwork of my days to be revealed as the mindful discovery of my True Self: an aspect of being-ness beyond the notion of suffering or lack of any kind.

Both/And (a view from the path of understanding)

In my delusion that I am separate from everything else,
I experience life as an either/or:
>It's either good or bad.
>I'm either good or bad.
>It's either beginning or ending.
>I'm either living or dying.
>It's either perfect or it's not.
>I'm either a success or a failure.

Living from the either/or is rigid, defined, and permanent:
>He's an asshole.
>I'll never live that down.
>It meant everything.

But the story is never that simple. . .
>He's an asshole,
>>but a lot of times he can be so cool, so supportive,
>>so great.
>I'll never live that down,
>>except here I am, and now things look so different
>>to me.
>It meant everything at the time,
>>but since then so much has happened and changed.

In this way, I can start to see that everything
is a BOTH/AND. I can see that everything is whole just
the way it is, that nothing is separate nor something I have
to reconcile before my heart can make peace with it:
>It was both a terrible thing that happened, and the
>birthplace for so many wonderful things since.

>I am both the one who said those awful things
>and the one who, learning from them, changed.

I am all of my experiences, both those I'd label as good and those I'd label as bad.

I am everything at once, creating my life as a great piece of music, one that needs every part:
    some moments I dance,
    some moments I wail, and
    some moments I rest.

I cannot control the thoughts, words, or deeds of others
any more than I can breathe for them. I can only take
responsibility for those things which are in my control.

I can control what I believe.
I can control my capacity to notice the thoughts
that rise from my beliefs.
I can control how I relate to emotions
that rise from my thoughts.
I can control my own actions
that rise from my emotions, even though I may fail in their
intended consequences or influence.
I can own my mistakes when they happen, and
I can do my best to make them right.

I can control my intent, and as such:

> May I be helpful.
> May I be honorable and accountable.
> May I build trust with others by being trustworthy.
> May I be kind and compassionate to myself
> and to others.
> May I listen and be patient.
> May I be mindful of my beliefs, thoughts,
> emotions, and actions, knowing that they will
> impact others and the world.
> May I see the interconnectedness of all things,
> recognizing how we're alike as much as honoring
> how we are unique.
> May I do my best to not cause harm.
> May I live this life fully, observing and leveling
> the walls I create in my own mind.
> May I love without conditions.
> May I give the best of myself completely.

May I see all things with a loving heart
that wants to help, rather than with a mind
that judges, defines, and compares.

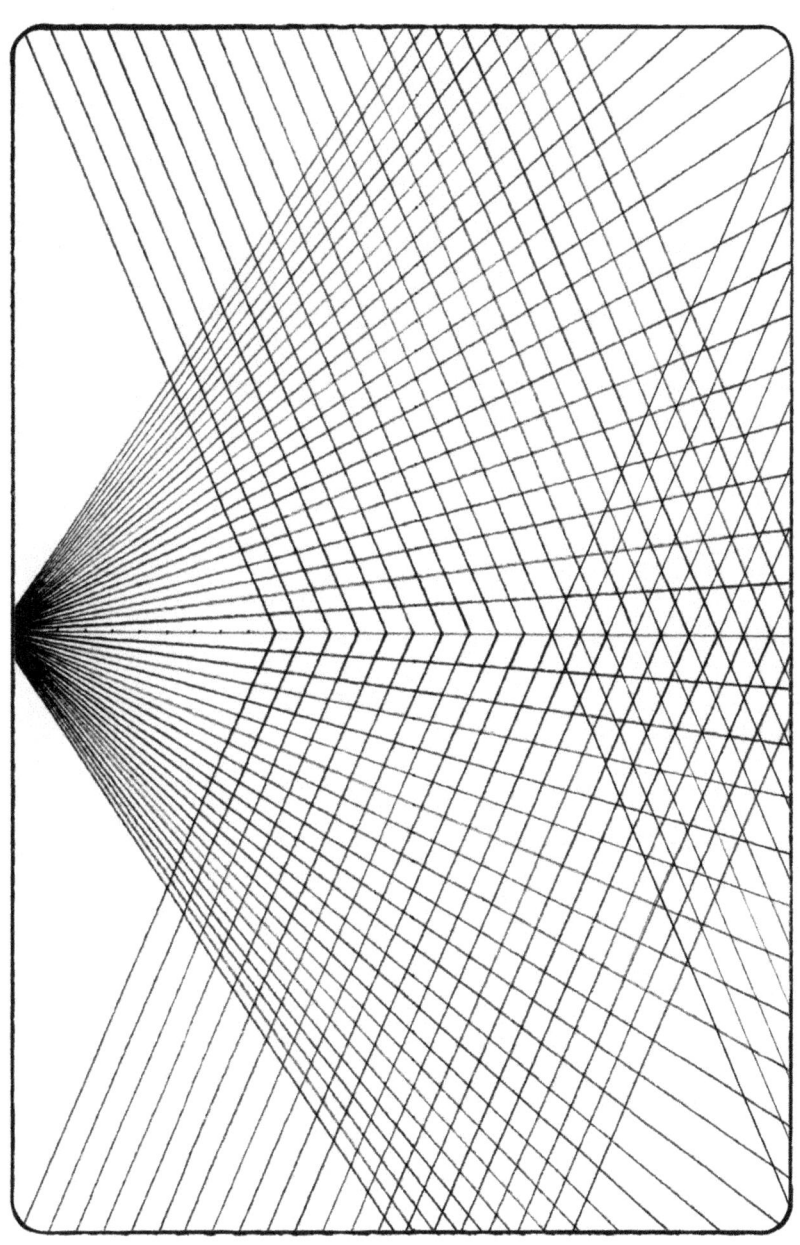

Finding the Person Under the Suffering

(on the path of speech)

My dad loved to passionately debate politics with me, and I hated every minute of it. He'd get loud. He'd get aggressive. He'd ask questions only to interrupt before I had two words out in response. I left every one of those debates with something ugly vibrating in the middle of my stomach. How could a guy I knew to be so great and smart and loving turn into such a bully? It's only years later that I can see that I never debated my dad—not even once. I debated his suffering.

I know that principles aren't innate, that what may appear to me like an objective moral imperative is really just the output from a lifetime's worth of conditioning, and when others' words or actions threaten my most deeply ingrained convictions (or support something I've learned to despise), they don't just threaten my values, they threaten my very identity. With this in mind:

Can I see the person underneath all of that conditioning and suffering?

Can I see that underneath even their most sacred values is someone who looks not just "kinda" like me, but exactly like me?

Can I see a human being who wants exactly what I want: to be safe, to live in peace, to know and experience love?

Can I connect with the deep aspects that are shared between us, instead of clashing with the surface details that can be so vastly different?

Can I feel compassion for the parts within them that suffer, even though those parts might drive actions that I find objectionable or harmful?

Towards the end of my dad's life, I used to experiment with this. Regardless of what he said, I chose to remember the incredible guy I loved under his inflammatory words, understanding that he was only using me as a safe target to express threats he felt towards a comfortable way of life that seemed to be falling away from him. I can't say that I ever "won" an argument with this approach, but by then it was no longer about winning, anyway. Without my fuel to add to his spark, his otherwise heated words cooled to shared questions about life, and then eventually to a sort of quiet calm.

While this may not resolve our society's many differences (not directly, at least), it does put us all together in the same boat. In some circumstances, this just might be enough (as it was with my dad). When it isn't, though, then maybe it's at least a good place from which to start.

020 The Psycle of Rebirth (on the path of action)

Do not overlook tiny good actions, thinking they are of no benefit;
even tiny drops of water in the end will fill a huge vessel.
Do not overlook negative actions merely because they are small;
however small a spark may be, it can burn down a haystack as big
as a mountain.
—The Buddha

If my actions are motivated by
    emotions that aren't mindful, driven by
        thoughts that aren't clear, grounded by
            beliefs that aren't rooted in wisdom,
then I will continue to suffer.

This is the psychological Wheel of Samsara: the cycle of
rebirth. With every new experience, I'm "reborn" to play out
my same old conditioned patterns.

Worse, it can contribute to larger suffering in the world.
As my suffering drives me to act poorly, it triggers

suffering in others,
which causes others to act poorly,
which triggers

But if my actions are driven by emotions that are peaceful,
which are born from thoughts that are clear,
which are created by beliefs that are rooted in wisdom,
then the Wheel of Samsara is transformed into the
Wheel of Nirvana, of Enlightenment.

Listening to a new voice within me,
I encounter the world mindfully—

> I am connected.
> I am courageous.
> I am compassionate.
> I am trustworthy.
> I am helpful.
> I am forgiving.

With every mindful action, I am reborn.
I'm given the opportunity to choose who I most want to be,
and in doing so, I not only impact my own life, but also
the lives of everyone around me, and ultimately

> I change the world.

021 Work/Life Balance (on the path of livelihood)

There is no such thing as work/life balance. It's all life.

My Ego Self can have a tendency to try to convince me that much of my value, potential, and purpose are tied to what I do and what I have, but that's just a story (and only as true as I choose it to be).

My True Self tells a different story. From the perspective of my True Self, I and everyone everywhere are expressions of Oneness itself. Each of us are Buddhas in the making (we just might not realize it yet). From this point of view, all occupations are equally esteemed: the fry cook, the CEO, the teacher, the toilet scrubber, the student, the stay-at-home parent, the celebrity, and the unemployed.

While I live, I will work, realizing that my job is just a vehicle that my True Self drives in service of its calling:

to connect, to feel, to love, to be.

My life's work will be a loving-kindness meditation in action. I'll use whatever jobs I hold as platforms to be helpful, creative, compassionate, and kind, no matter what my job description or role is.

Each day, the more stress, disillusion, selfishness, and disconnection I encounter, the more opportunity I have to do something truly unique and special: to be the exact kind of person that the world needs most.

In this way:

> When others lose their cool, I'll do my best
> to keep mine. When I lose an opportunity
> or fail, I'll do my best to learn from it. When
> I inevitably run into a difficult customer,
> boss, colleague, or partner, I'll do my best
> to remember that others' poor behavior is just
> a symptom of suffering, not villainy; I'll
> do my best to listen. When I run into questionable
> ethics or poor treatment, I'll do my best
> to stand squarely in a place that is honorable.
> When others fail to lead, I'll do my best to step up.

Imagine the impact that might come from a life-long career of this!

022

Feeding the Wolf (on the path of effort)

An old man was quietly staring at the flames of the fire he had built with his granddaughter when she asked, "Grandpa, what are you thinking about?" The old man replied, "I'm thinking of the two wolves who fight inside of me. One is courageous, open-hearted, kind, trustworthy, and good. The other is selfish, greedy, impatient, and consumed with hatred. Every day, they snarl, growl, bite, and claw at each other inside of me." With eyes like saucers, the little girl looked at her grandfather and asked, "Which one will win?" The old man replied, "The one that I feed."
—Indigenous American Folktale

_____

Every day, I can feed the good wolf inside of me.

Every morning, I can renew my intent and remind myself of the person I most want to be, guarding my mind from thoughts that might otherwise threaten to carry me away from who I most truly am.

When troubled by unhelpful thoughts, I can mindfully inquire into the nature of my thinking, and work to choose how I react from a place of understanding and love.

Every day, I can develop the goodness that lives within me already.

I can remind myself that the fullness of life can be realized through the quality of my being much more than from the fruits of my actions.

I can remind myself that every tiny step is a rediscovery of who I am. Instead of viewing my effort as a burden (or even as "a practice"), I can see it as a conscious choice to live with purpose and meaning.

Every evening, I can cultivate and preserve the good that already lives within me.

I can notice the many small acts of kindness everywhere, flowing from the good wolves within others.

I can welcome into my heart the wondrous beauty right outside of my own window—the earth, the water, the sky, the plants, and the animals—and allow their song to harmonize with my own: all our heads thrown back and howling at the same moon as one, all of us discovering mysterious truths much deeper than anything we could possibly find alone.

hmm. (on the path of concentration)

I'm not doing anything. I'm not attaining. I'm not changing.
I'm not accomplishing.

> I'm just breathing,
> just feeling,
> just watching.

I can fix stuff later, but for now, I'm just sitting,
just watching—just seeing what's there.

The thoughts come:

> floating in,
> barging and crashing,
> whispering,
> accusing,
> making fun of me,
> shaming me.

I touch them all with the simplest acknowledgement, "hmm,"
and I let them drift away as I return to my breath, my
home base.

> I'm breathing.
> I'm feeling.
> I'm watching.

I can fix stuff later, I'm just sitting, I'm just watching—
They're there whether I know it or not (and I'd rather know).
They're thoughts. They're conditioning. They don't define
me. I see them, and in seeing them, I offer a nod of "hmm"
as I reconnect to this very moment, my True Home, and
I let them go.

They come, and I let them go.

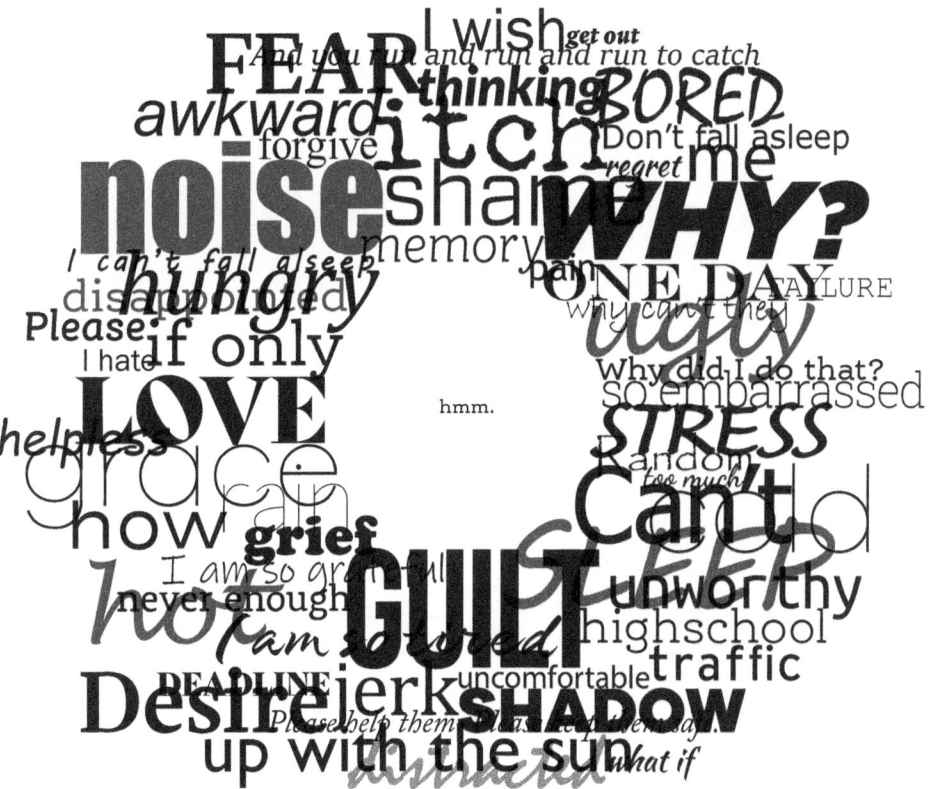

When I notice that I'm suffering; when I'm experiencing emotions such as anger, anxiety, guilt, depression, boredom, despair, insecurity, embarrassment, regret, envy, annoyance, hopelessness, stress, depression, panic, rage, confusion, bewilderment, disgust, unhappiness, shame, irritability, jealousy, exasperation, hostility, frustration, isolation, neglect, misery, dismay, nervousness, horror, hate, mortification, inadequacy, inferiority, terror, hysteria, revulsion, agony, disillusionment, gloom, empty-heartedness...

They all seem to be driven by some variation of the thought:

> "(My)Life is not what it should be."

The thoughts are usually much more well-crafted than this: I use more words, and some of them are really impressive, expensive words. I also tend to include a whole bunch of ideas, reasons, justifications, etc., but if I'm being honest (and why wouldn't I be?), they all basically boil down to the following phrase:

> "(My)Life is not what it should be."

When I search for why it is that I think this way, I find that my thoughts always seem to be grounded by some variation of the belief that:

> "A good life is based on what I do and/or what I have, and right now, I don't do what I should be doing, and/or I don't have what I should have, and therefore my life isn't what it should be."

It's important to note that the variations that this belief takes include most all verb forms of "to do" and/or "to have"—for instance, the belief may rest in some past or future case of either verb, such as "A good life is one where I shouldn't have done what I did," or ". . .

where I'm able to have what I'll never be able to have."
And so on.

Here's an example:
One time, I was sitting at my desk at work, rushing like crazy
to finish something that was due that afternoon, when
a manager (who I really didn't like) came out of nowhere and
gave me a new assignment that was "critical" and "urgent"
and then started to talk and talk about it while the clock
hands seemed to both speed up and slow down at the same
time, and I remember feeling hot in my cheeks and tight
in my neck and shoulders and my fists balled up underneath
my desk and I was flooded with emotions like anger, despair,
and stress, but the one that was easily the most painful was
a visceral feeling of being trapped (it was sort of like
a terrible blend of panic, shame, and powerlessness). Driving
these emotions were many thoughts, such as "Oh man, do
I hate this guy!" and "There's no way I can do all of this!" and
"Why me?" and "I quit!" and many other "greatest hits," but

> the GRAND DADDY THOUGHT that ruled them all
> was, "My life is not my own."

See how my story fits my template like a glass slipper fits
a certain princess' foot?

Emotion =
  Trapped (panic, shame, powerlessness)
Thought =
  "My life is not my own." (I think that's fairly easy
  to translate to "My life is not what it should
  be," right?)
Belief =
  A good life is one where I perform highly
  in a job that I love with really amazing leaders
  where we do really great work making the world
  a better place AND I DON'T HAVE ANY OF THAT.

So now what?

Well, clarity is a wonderful thing, but it doesn't exactly feel amazing on its own. It's wonderful to recognize my (very human) strategies for how I tend to experience suffering, but I'm left with an important question:

Would I choose this experience?

Is how I feel, think, and believe something that I would choose, or is there another belief that I hold, one that is every bit as true as the one that generated my suffering, but instead generates a different, helpful, or useful thought that results in an emotional state that aligns with how I'd most like to feel, given the circumstances in front of me.

Choice is an important distinction here, because no emotions, thoughts, or beliefs are "bad" or "good" in and of themselves. If I experience the loss of someone close to me, then I would choose to experience emotions like grief and sadness, even though they aren't pleasant. They're part of being human and processing experiences in life that are painful, but when my state of being isn't based on something clear—on something that I would choose—then maybe I have an opportunity to explore reorienting myself to something different.

What might I choose? Given any circumstances that I might encounter, how would I most like to feel? For myself, my answers always tend to sound something like:

I'd most like to feel connected, peaceful, content, and grateful. I'd like to feel whole. If happiness is present, then I'd like to feel joyful. If suffering is present, then I'd like to feel compassionate.
I'd like to feel like I'm one with life.
I'd like to feel like I flow.

So, what thought(s) might drive an emotional experience like this? When I think of times when I have felt this way, they were all driven by some variation of the thoughts:

"(My)Life is amazing," or
"(My)Life is incredible," or
"(My)Life is beautiful."

And these thoughts always seem to be grounded by some variation of a belief that I can't always seem to put neatly into words, but that I might be able to find by looking around and asking myself,

"Well, is it?
Is life amazing?
Is it incredible?
Is it beautiful?"

So it becomes a test:
an experiment on connecting with what's right in front of me, and seeing what happens next. Now, please don't get me wrong, there's no doubt that life certainly includes suffering and horror and injustice and tragedy, but in this experiment, can I give myself permission to set these to the side for just a moment? Can I explore the possibilities that emerge when I truly investigate the life around me—maybe even outside of my very own window? What do I see? What do I hear? What, at this very moment, do I experience?

025 Well, Is It?

Look around. Listen.
What's there?
 a tree, a person, a building, a song, a whir, a rhythm,
 sounds of traffic, or the wind, or birds, or an ocean,
 or a garbage truck, or people talking or even yelling . . .
 See it? Hear it?

Isn't it wild that there is anything at all?
Isn't it amazing to notice it?
And to get to notice it?

Isn't life amazing?

Lift the veil of what usually goes unnoticed, the routine
and the banal.
What's there?
 Feel the air outside you become you as you breathe
 and transform it, only to offer it again. Feel yourself
 beating your heart and know the miracle inside you
 that has been constant without effort, flowing just like
 springtime or a stream or a blade of grass or a star. Feel
 the warmth of the huge glowing orange ball in the sky
 that every one of us twirls around day and night.

Isn't it wild that there is anything at all?
Isn't it incredible to notice it?
And to get to notice it?

Isn't life incredible?

Remember everyone who has ever loved you, cared for you,
or helped you. Remember everyone you have ever loved,
cared for, or helped.

Remember them and feel them—
   feel them like they are right here—
   teachers, friends, funny dogs, ornery cats, brothers,
   sisters, mothers, fathers, strangers with kind words,
   long lost pals, confidants.

Remember all that's shared—
   a joke, a really great movie, a freshly baked cookie,
   a good hard cry, a gentle breeze, a warm day, a warm
   fire, a flower, a stream.

Isn't it beautiful to know them?
Isn't it beautiful to have known and to be known by them?

   Isn't life beautiful?

Someone (outside of me) does or says something

BadUglyHarmfulDeceitfulVillainous

First, I sense it. It shows up as the slightest of feelings—
like the color of a feeling, a tone. My mind takes it—waters
it, feeds it, helps it grow—until it blossoms into something
that I can truly call my own with

DistasteDisgustAntipathyLoathing
(Aversion)

And I know I don't want it and that I'll do whatever I can
to stay away from it, until life finally lets me up when
something happens (outside of me), something

PleasantSweetDelightfulAmiableHeroic

And I water it, feed it, speak to it to help it grow until it
blossoms into something that I can truly call my own with

WantingGraspingDesiringCraving
(Attachment)

And I want it so badly and I'll do whatever I can to get
or keep it, and the only thing that saves me from this
pain of wanting is when

And on and on and on and on and on and on and on and

These are the 10,000 things of life. All of them making
me dig for treasure where every gold coin I might find sits
on broken rocks and shards of glass, and in my constant,
sweaty, exhausting digging, I forget to look up! I forget
that above the swirling

DramaComedyHorrorTragedyFarce is

SomethingElse?
IsItSomeoneElse?
IsItMe?

Who seems to know something different

SomethingVastExpansiveTimeless

And it all is suddenly so obvious that it shoves the breath
from my lungs,

WhisperingShoutingShakingTelling
me that

The 10,000 things are teachers, showing me over and over
that every

AversionAttachment
is a
DeadendTrickConBamboozleHeadfake

that I'm doing to myself in my own mind; that none
of it happens outside of me without my say-so; that when
I brush it all away like sand from a mosaic floor, that what
is left is something

VastExpansiveTimeless,

like love?maybe?
like peace?maybe?
like light?maybe?
like being awake.

027 The Arrows of Pain and Suffering

Life includes pain—
illnesses, accidents, tragedies, disasters—
I feel their impacts, as do people I love, people I struggle
with, and all beings everywhere.

The Buddha taught that these painful experiences are like
being shot with an arrow, but the stories I tell myself about
these painful experiences are like being shot with a second
arrow. In this way, the first arrow is the arrow of pain, and
the second is the arrow of suffering:

I receive painful news about myself or someone I love
    (the arrow of pain),
and I blame myself for not doing what I should have to prevent it
    (the arrow of suffering).

I lose a relationship with someone
    (the arrow of pain),
and I tell myself that I'm not worthy of being loved or accepted
    (the arrow of suffering).

I'm let go from my job
    (the arrow of pain),
and I'm filled with feelings of insecurity and anger
    (the arrows of suffering),
and I chastise myself for feeling insecure and angry for
not being able to handle it better
    (another arrow of suffering),
and I tell myself how badly people will think of me for
losing my job
    (more arrows of suffering),
and I'm filled with anxiety and dread about losing
my health insurance and my car and I'm certain that
Christmas will be ruined
    (even more arrows of suffering—I'm starting
    to look like a pin cushion).

The Buddha's wisdom is simple (even if it isn't always easy):
Focus on the first arrow. Take care of the first arrow.
Let go of the stories. Let go of the suffering.

One arrow is enough.

028　One Coin, Two Sides

By some yet unanswered mystery,
I am here and I am conscious of it:
an aperture of the universe,
the whole thing, experiencing itself through me.

I feel the sun and joy and love.
　　I grow and watch others grow.
　　I thrive and watch others thrive.
　　I am born and watch as others are born.

And for this wonder, I pay the price.

I feel the cold and sorrow and loss.
　　I age and watch others age.
　　I get sick and watch others get sick.
　　I know that I will die and watch others die.

I know others' suffering exactly as I know my own—
　　I see it in a child or an animal,
　　I see it in a friend or loved one,
　　I see it in a stranger or even an enemy.

And I find myself moved.
　　And I see myself as not alone.
　　And I watch as countless arms reach out in response:
　　the nurse, the teacher, the aid worker, the friend, the
　　parent, the counselor, the hug, the shoulder, the sitting
　　quietly, the listening.

And I feel it within me,
　　And I know it is within everyone:
　　As true as suffering is, so is love, so is care, so is compassion.

And I only know one because I know,
deeply, intimately,
the other.

029 Compassion Is an Action

It was a video of a man hurting an animal, and my reaction was visceral. I wanted to immediately hurt that man just as he was hurting that animal, and my feelings of impotence to do so nearly equaled my wrath.

The Buddha teaches that, without exception, all beings deserve compassion, but I was left drained. I couldn't understand how to feel compassion for that man because I couldn't imagine how that man could possibly deserve it.

I watched the video again. It seems crazy, but I had to. I had to find something in it that might make sense to me. Maybe it was staged. Maybe there was some justifiable reason behind his actions that I'd find if I only watched closely enough. I had to try. I had to find something that could somehow lessen the raw molten anger and hatred that seemed to have swallowed me whole.

I noticed that the man's surroundings appeared absolutely impoverished, and in seeing this, I recognized that I had no frame of reference for what it was like to live as he seemed to be living. How did he grow up? Who taught him how to think, feel, and act? What kind of culture was it? How does he live now? Does he have a family? Does he have children? Do they count on him? What if their lives somehow depend on him doing the exact thing that I automatically want to judge as unforgivably cruel?

If the people I love more than I love my own life were starving and needed me to hurt an animal for their survival, wouldn't I do the same as that man?

Could it be possible that he has a worldview where his actions are correct and justified, exactly like I have one where they are not?

Had I grown up where he grew up, had I lived like he lived, had I learned what he learned, is it possible that I would think and act exactly as he does?

Is it possible that the only difference between us is where we were born?

Could I be him?

In some way, am I him already?

What if I were to open my heart for that man, even if I don't really understand what that means?

Nothing Is Never Not a Beginning

I loved my dad very much, and sometimes I struggled to like
him. He was a wonderful person and sometimes he was
a bully. He supported me in countless ways just as he also
did not. He loved my family deeply and worked incredibly
hard to provide a good life for us, just as he sometimes
caused pain born from his own suffering that had followed
him since he was a kid.

My mom, my brother, my wife, and I were all very quiet
during the final breaths of his life. I meditated but was
distracted by the distinct sensation of being pushed
backward. It was very strange: I was sitting on the edge
of my chair, only a few inches from his bedside, and I kept
feeling like I was being pushed back by some gentle warm
current. I assumed it was me but found myself actively
tightening my stomach to remain upright.

At the moment I realized that there was not going to be
another inbreath, I had a sort of vision—I'm not sure what
else I might call it. In one single instant, I saw his entire life
as one complete work, like his last breath was a bookend
to a story I was able to read in one gulp. I saw every decision
he made, every failure, every success, every lucky turn,
every anxiety. I felt every time he looked forward
to something, just like I do. I watched his hopes come
to fruition and also fall short, just like they do for me. I saw
him worry about his family, just like I do, and I watched
him try to navigate the waters of what's best for the people
around him, just like I do. I saw him just like me. I saw his
whole life like my own life, and for one incredible flash, this
realization tunneled like light surrendering to a black hole,
and I saw him not like me, but *as* me. I don't mean this
as an analogy or a metaphor—I mean this literally:
I saw him (felt him?) as me.

I looked up and I thought of the trees across the hospital parking lot and the bed and the chairs and the basket of snacks from earlier and the nurses and everyone I know and have known and everyone I'll never meet nor know, and everything in all places was exactly One, and without asking or trying, I was filled with certainty and gratitude and love. In that moment, there was no sin or transgression that required forgiveness or even the suggestion of it. I felt held somehow, and everything became infinitely spacious and undeniably complete, as though someone had called out to me about something they needed me to know.

Compelled to understand, I entered the seminary about a month later. Up until the very moment I took the Precepts, I could feel my twenty-year-old self looking at me strangely, asking, "We're doin' what now?" I still can't help but marvel at how my life doesn't look at all like what I may have once predicted, and how I find myself so very thankful for every painful inadequacy, every crushing embarrassment, every disappointment, every failure, and every loss that led to exactly now.

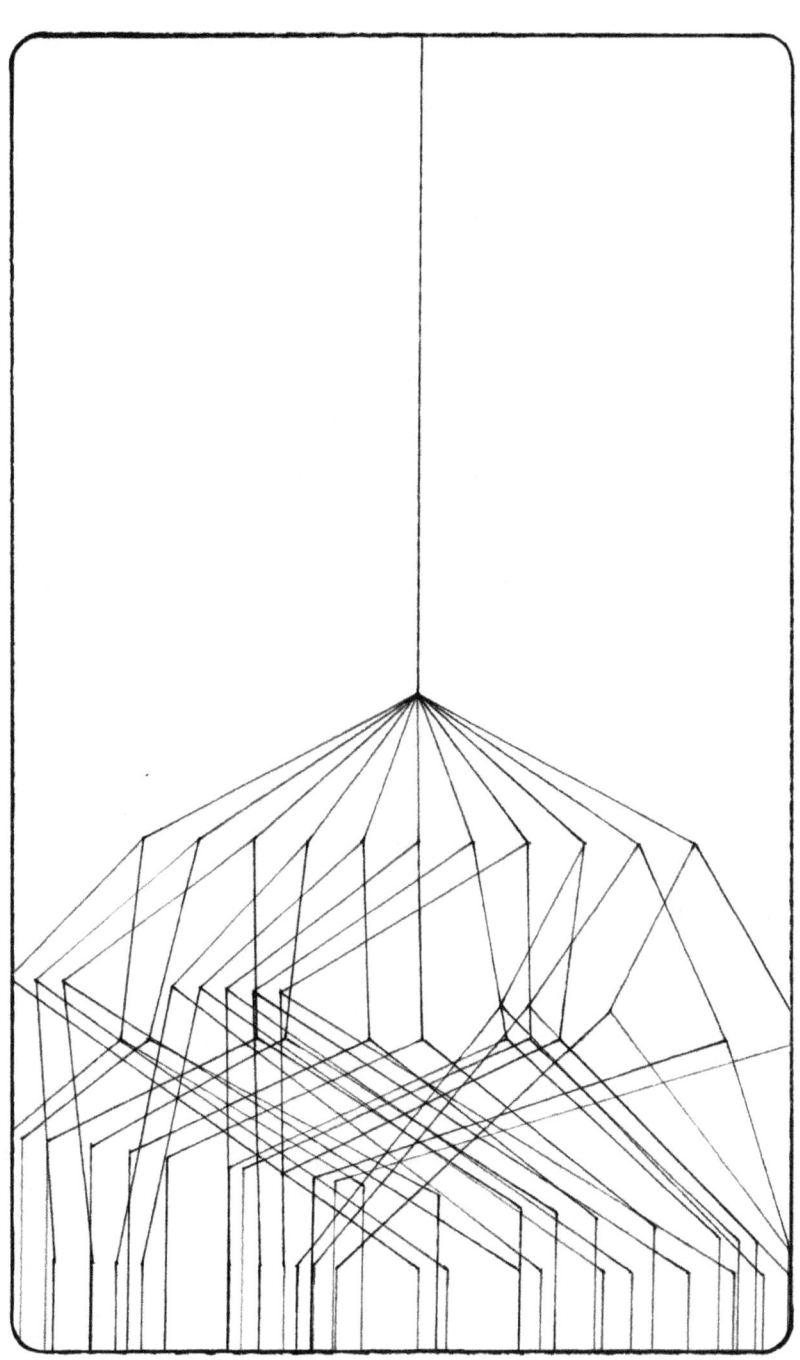

031   Is That So?

Once upon a time, long ago, a young unwed daughter of a well-respected family realized in shock and horror that she was with child. When her parents questioned her about the identity of the father, the young girl, in utter distress and shame, panicked and named the beloved and respected Zen monk, Hakuin. The infuriated parents immediately dashed to the monastery and angrily accused Hakuin, loudly berating and shaking their fingers in front of all who were present.

To their accusations, Hakuin only replied, "Is that so?"

When the child was born, the girl's parents took the baby girl to Hakuin and left her with him to care for. Again, they chided him for what he had done, crying "The fault is yours and so is the burden!"

As Hakuin took the tiny child in his arms, he simply and quietly replied, "Is that so?"

As the months passed, Hakuin lovingly cared for the little girl, laughing with her every morning, walking with her in his arms every afternoon, singing sweetly to her every sunset, and dancing gently with her every night when she sleeplessly cried.

After a year, the young village girl could not bear her guilt any longer and confessed to her parents that she had lied—that the father of the baby was not Hakuin, but a young man who worked at the fish market. Mortified, the family rushed to the monastery and wailed for Hakuin's forgiveness. As they sobbed and took the child from Hakuin, they explained the truth, admonishing themselves for their rash behavior and lamentable conduct.

With great compassion, Hakuin simply replied, "Is that so?"

032 The Flower

The flower is empty without the stem.
The stem is empty without the roots.
The roots are empty without the water.
The water is empty without the sky.
The sky is empty without the sun.

They are all empty without my knowing them.

One is empty without zero.
Somethingness is empty without nothingness.
Emotion is empty without thought.

There is nothing that exists in and of itself.
Everything seen as separate is, in truth, a relationship.
Everything seen as static is, in truth, an evolution.

In Zen, Oneness is defined as "not two."

This is the truth of who I am:
I am the relationship with all there is.
I am changed as it changes, and as I change,
I change it in turn.

Light as a Feather

I asked her, "Given the exact same situation again, the one that caused all of the anxiety, insecurity, and hurt, how would you like to feel?" I was expecting an emotion, something like "peaceful" or "content," so when she gave her reply, it kind of stopped me in my tracks and I thought to myself, "Yeah, wow, me too. That's how I'd want to be, too." What she said was, "I want to flow, man."

In flow,
Unburdened by the weight of past and future,
Buoyed by an awakened heart and mind,
Moved by a calling beyond words and scriptures,
Effort becomes effortless,
And state of being becomes the state of doing.

The painter is the brush and the canvas.
The archer is the arrow and the target.
The athlete is the ground and the air.
The leader is the policy and the change.
The teacher is the lesson and the student.

Can I be that?
Can I level the walls of my mind?
Can I feel heaviness as advice to move in another way?
Can I surrender to everything that is this moment?
Can I be light as a feather?
Can I flow?

034 Bob's Tattoos

My friend Bob has "Breathe In" tattooed on his left wrist and "Breathe Out" on his right.

He says that they remind him that he entered the world with his first breath in, and that he'll exit it with his last breath out, but that what matters most is what he does in between.

He says he wonders how many breaths he's taken of which he was actually aware, and how many he'd grade as high-quality.

He wonders if he's even breathing at this very moment.

He remembers that his daughters were reluctant to go with him to get his tattoos. He says that they're both covered in tattoos now.

He says that he was once embarrassed about his tattoos, at least in some settings, and that he'd try to hide or cover them in business meetings. He says that he doesn't do that anymore.

He says that any questions or glances (no matter how sideways) give him an opportunity to connect with people at a level that people don't normally go to out of the gate.

He says "Breathe In" reminds him of holding his children as they took their first breaths. He says "Breathe Out" reminds him of holding his mom as she took her last.

He says that if he closes his eyes, he can go back to those moments and feel them as though they're happening now: all of their joy and pain.

He says that if he stops breathing, he stops living, so his number one priority is to keep breathing for as long as he can.

He says that it sounds simple, but that it's just too easy to forget.

He says he guesses that's why he's got it written on his left and right wrists.

I remember listening to friends talk about their times spent as emergency room chaplains.

I remember them talking about singing Christian hymns at the requests of those in their last moments, and about walking into the dimly lit rooms of folks who had just passed, the families quietly surrounding the bed.

I remember them talking about sitting with people directly outside of the medical bay as someone they loved battled for life, teams of caregivers rushing in and out of the room, voices raised and urgent.

I remember them talking about embracing caregivers as they cried because they did everything they possibly could, but were unable to halt the stubborn insistence of death.

I remember them talking about intercepting frantic and terrified parents who only knew that their child was brought to the ER, but didn't yet know that their last moments together had already passed.

I remember them talking about doing these things over and over, every day, over and over.

I remember feeling it in my throat and stomach and chest. I remember it all seeming impossible to me, wondering how in these circumstances there could be any combination of words that didn't seem wholly inadequate at best and insulting or damaging at worst. I remember asking them both,

How do you walk into those rooms?
How do you know what to say?

and I remember their answer seeming to come in unison:

"I don't know."

They said that there were no prepared answers that could be helpful in those moments, but instead,

they moved aside the notion that they knew anything at all, they opened themselves completely to what was present, bearing witness to whatever appeared, and they allowed themselves to be spoken through.

_/_

The First Tenet is Not-Knowing
This is wisdom (prajna).

My temptation (my conditioning) is to automatically react, but in doing so, I'm being controlled. I'm unconscious. I'm relying on automatic solutions that may not be effective nor helpful.

> With Great Doubt, I place all that I know to the side
> of the experience, allowing myself to be open
> to whatever comes.

> I choose to honor the experience as wholly new.
> I choose to doubt my reactive answers,
> I choose to set them aside.
> I choose to clear my mind so that it may be free.

The Second Tenet is Bearing Witness
This is awareness (samadhi).

I am fully present to what is. I am wholly without judgment. I choose to listen with a heart that wants to know, not through the veil of my own projections.

> With Great Faith, I allow myself to be at one with
> the experience, completely connected to it.

> I am fully present and listening intuitively with
> my whole being to understand and learn.
> I am open to whatever appears, whatever it may be.

The Third Tenet is Right Action

This is virtue (sila).

Having moved through the gates of not-knowing and bearing witness, any and all that happens next is emergent, born from exactly what the moment asks of it.

With Great Courage, I allow my True Self to step forward.

If I speak, I am spoken through.
If I act, I am acted through.
If I do nothing at all, then it is the very highest quality of nothing.

037 Great Doubt

I have no idea how I open and close my hand,
and yet I do it without thought.

I drive for miles and miles and don't remember
any of it, and yet I safely navigate every turn.

I have no idea what love is,
and yet I know exactly what it is in my heart.

I have no idea what an experience is,
and yet I experience the world.

I have no idea why I came to be,
and yet I am.

I rely on what I don't know much more than what I do know.

Every moment—without understanding or realizing it—I call
on wisdom that is far beyond my conscious mind.
In practicing Great Doubt,

I set aside all that I know and I open myself to all
of the knowledge that exists beyond my thoughts.

I open myself to microexpressions of emotion
and cues that are far too subtle or fast for my
mind to catch and process consciously.

I address what's in front of me, armed not only
with the answers that I carry in the awareness
of my mind, but with the vast intelligence of my
entire being.

I bring all of the mystery with me.

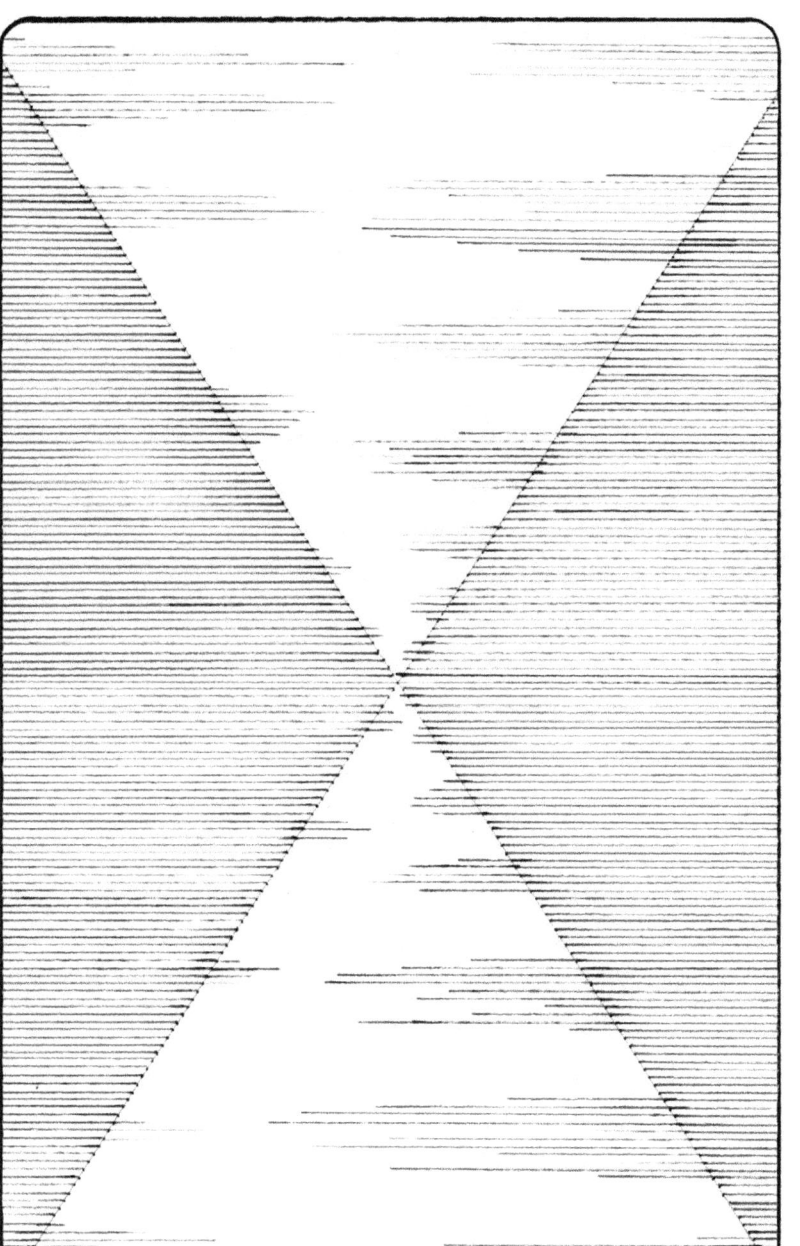

Great Faith

I was drowning in depression and despair. It was about
10 p.m. on a Monday night some years ago and I wanted
to be done. I wanted to die. I was standing outside with our
little dog, and by some miracle, a pinprick of light broke
through just enough to move me to whisper out to the air,

> I could really use a hand right now.

The next day, a friend who I hadn't talked to for a long time
called out of the blue, and later that day, I wrote one measure
of music that I thought was okay. They were small things, but
I felt lifted.

That evening, I was reflecting on how badly I felt just the
day before, and how crazy it was that I felt a little better
today, when I suddenly remembered my whisper to the air,
and I wondered:

Did something actually help me?

And it dawned on me that this has happened before.
I'd been low, I asked for help, and then something
unpredictable happened—something changed that turned
me ever so slightly in a new direction, creating possibilities
that hadn't been there before. The enormous difference,
though, was that this time I noticed it. This time, I didn't
take it for granted as mere coincidence. In that moment,
it became quite certain to me:

Something helped me.

In practicing Great Faith,

I choose to set skepticism aside and
to see coincidence and random occurrence
as the offering of a mystery that I may never
fully understand.

I set aside all semblance of judgment,
abandoning labels like "good" or "bad" and
greeting all that occurs with equanimity.

I become the moment, itself.

I bear witness to what is.

039 Great Courage

Courage and fearlessness are not synonymous.

Fearlessness is the absence of fear, and at the risk
of boasting, I've done many, many things in my life with
the complete absence of fear.
For example,
> I've eaten countless bowls of cereal without one iota
> of fear in my heart.
> I've mopped dozens of floors, dusted tons of furniture, and
> vacuumed hundreds of rooms without any apprehension.
> I've strode out to the mailbox and retrieved the mail
> without a single wisp of dread.

Courage, though, is different.
Courage is being afraid, but doing it anyway, and I haven't
done one thing of significance in my life that didn't include
at least some amount of fear.
For example,
> I was nervous as all get-out when I asked my wife out on
> our first date.
> I was scared out of my mind when we decided to move
> our family to another country.
> I was afraid that I wasn't worthy when I took the
> Precepts and Vows to be an ordained Buddhist priest
> and teacher.

These moments are among those that have truly shaped the
story of my life, encompassing what matters most to me,
and every one of them included fear, worry, doubt, anxiety,
and even dread.

In practicing Great Courage,

I know that I'm stepping into something that scares me, and yet I choose to do it anyway.

I am resolute in my intent and am not swayed by any easier path. I am immovable.

I allow my True Self, the me I most want to be in this world, to guide my actions and my speech.

I step forward.

Picture a great lion waking. Picture it surveying.
   (that's you)

Picture its face. Picture its golden eyes gleaming.
   (that's you)

Picture its yawn. Picture its teeth, each one like a warning—
like an inevitability.
   (that's you)

Picture its daggered paws and rippling shoulders like the
waves of a vast sea.
   (that's you)

Picture its mane granting the wind permission to comb
it and its tail's dance a nod to every creature who now
understands: "The lion is awake!"
   (that's you)

Breathe in fully. Take in all of the air. Imagine its energy
filling every space and every crevasse. Imagine your
in-breath bending all of the savanna grass towards you.

Hold it for a moment. Feel its impatience as it waits to deliver
its bold and primal proclamation to all things everywhere:

   I am here.

Now shake the trees from the earth and the birds from their
perches and

   send

         it

             out.

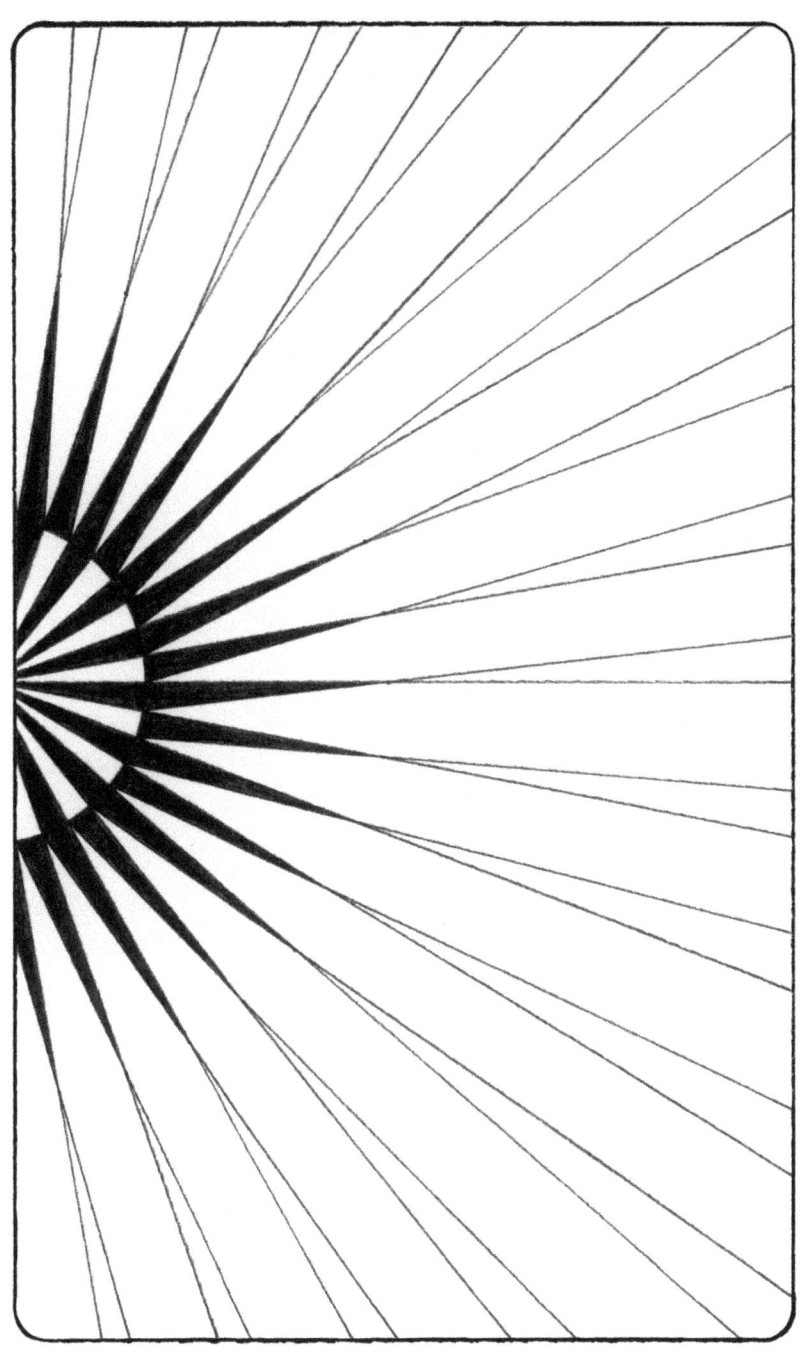

041 Make Tea

Once upon a time, there was a tea master who worked in the service of a great Samurai Lord, and whose tea ceremony was without equal. In his seemingly simple practice, he was able to produce a calmness of mind, clarity, and presence that was palpable and contagious, greatly affecting all who were present. The Samurai Lord was so taken with the tea master's abilities that he bestowed upon him the rank of samurai and gifted him the traditional two swords to wear in his obi.

One day, while walking through the streets of Edo, the tea master encountered a fearsome warrior at a bridge. Without thinking, the tea master stepped aside to allow the warrior to pass, causing the warrior to exclaim, "Who is this who wears the swords of a samurai but so meekly steps aside? You're no samurai. You're a coward and an imposter, and I challenge you to a duel tomorrow morning at this very bridge. If you truly are a samurai, then you'll at least die honorably, but if you're not, then you'll die like a quivering rabbit and bring shame to your family and ancestors."

Stricken and terrified by the thought that his certain death could bring shame to his family, the tea master ran to his lord and asked him to please teach him how to die honorably. The lord looked at the tea master and said, "Of course, I'll help you. I'll teach you exactly what you need to know, but first, please perform your tea ceremony for me one last time."

When the ceremony had ended, the lord said to the tea master, "Tomorrow, when you face this warrior, imagine with all that you are that you're performing this very same tea ceremony. Bring with you this same presence of mind to the drawing of your sword."

The next day at the bridge, the tea master did exactly as his lord advised. As the warrior drew his sword, so did the tea master, bringing the same calmness of mind and presence as he had practiced over a lifetime of performing the tea ceremony.

Immediately and at once, the warrior realized that he had made a dreadful mistake. Clearly, he had arrogantly and stupidly challenged someone far beyond his own skill. Trembling, he bowed deeply and apologized profusely for making such an egregious error, and with as much dignity as he could muster, quickly made his escape.

The Eight Worldly Winds

The winds blow—

> gain and loss,
> fame and disgrace,
> praise and blame,
> pleasure and pain.

The Buddha teaches,
"These eight winds spin after the world, and the world spins
after them."

It is within my nature to chase them as I am chased by them:

> To win.
> To prove my worth.
> To rise above ceilings of my own design.

But they are winds, and as such

> they come
> and go
> and come
> and go.

And I know that there is something else within me as well,

> Something that is also my nature:
> Something beyond the need to win
> or to prove
> or to rise above.

Can I see it revealed in a glance or a laugh or a song
or a fragrance or a touch?

Can I see it as real as anything else I know about myself
or the world, a Mountain of Truth that no wind can move?

Can I see the ground upon which all things are born?

Can I know that I am that?

043 Humility

I was 23 when I first met my teacher, Julia. For our lesson,
I had prepared the first Brahms rhapsody, and as I started
to play, I let loose with everything I had:

> every storm's gale and gust,
> every elephant's siren and stomp,
> every whale's bellow and breach,
> every electric atom of a 23-year-old poised
> on the precipice of their own imagined greatness.

At the first natural break in the music, Julia raised her
hand, thanked me, and asked me to stand up from the
bench. For the next three hours we carefully worked
on how to properly sit at the piano.

044 The Holy Light Switch

It is in this way that we must train ourselves:
By liberation of the self through love,
We will cultivate love,
We will make it our vehicle and our basis,
We will take a stand upon it, store it up, and thoroughly set it going.
—The Buddha

Love is not a contract. Love is not quid pro quo where you give it to me and only then do I give it to you in return.

No, love is more like an electrical circuit. I flip the switch, completing the circuit, and love naturally flows, lighting every room and beyond, and simultaneously returning to me like a great bright heavenly lamp.

Flipping this Holy Light switch doesn't depend on anyone or anything else. It doesn't depend on what I'm wearing, where I am, how I describe myself, my past actions, or my future prospects: I simply give the light away, and the light comes back to me.

How it happens may be a surprise—it may not come back from my "target" (which may seem disappointing), but that's the old way of thinking, the quid pro quo way of thinking. This is different. This is a blast outward to everyone everywhere, and in this way, it is mine the moment I offer it.

And so I offer it.

045

Butsudan

A beautiful sunrise over the cymbals of ocean waves.
A spacious, clear, and starry night sky.
A wordless walk shared with deer and fox through
an autumnal forest.
An awe-inspiring vista across miles and miles of vast
rolling terrain.

In these experiences, time seems to stop—worry and regret
melts away, and something infinite and sacred is revealed.

But life moves. Life gets busy and hectic and stressful.
In the swirl of it all, I forget that the profound and sacred
is not reserved just for rare moments and distant places,
but it is always within me.

In my home, on a small table in a small room, there
is an altar: a butsudan. It is my physical place of refuge,
reflection, and prayer.

In the center of the table, there is a stack of stones.
I gathered them at my favorite hiking spots, and they serve
to reach into my heart and connect me to that "something"
which is bigger than myself.

To the left of the stones and a little behind is a small bowl
of water, reminding me of the source and flow of all life and
that my body, too, is mostly this very same stuff.

To the left of the stones and a little in front is a flower.
I allow the flower to fully wilt and petals to drop before
I replace it with a fresh one. The flower reminds me of both
the beauty of life and the change that is inherent within it.

In front of the stones is a small bowl of sand for burning incense.
The scent of the incense reminds me of life's joys, and the
rising smoke represents my intentions spreading outward into
the world around me, made manifest through my actions.

To the right of the stones and a little behind is a singing bowl and mallet. With a gentle touch of the mallet, I remind myself that this sound is me—my True Self, ringing out into the universe.

To the right of the stones and a little in front is a candle. With each lighting, I'm reminded of my calling toward igniting the flame of enlightenment and ending suffering for myself and all sentient beings.

To the unknowing eye, it's just a table with some tchotchkes on it, but this would woefully miss its true nature. Looking more closely, one might get a glimpse of what is really there: a beautiful sunrise over the cymbals of ocean waves, a spacious, clear, and starry night sky, a wordless walk shared with deer and fox through an autumnal forest, and an awe-inspiring vista across miles and miles of vast rolling terrain.

046

The Elephant in the Room

The instructor, some guy named Joe, looked around at the group of us in the conference room and asked, "What do you think: Is seeing believing, or is believing seeing?" We sort of murmured some pretty noncommittal responses for a few moments before he held out his fist and said, "Well, I can make an elephant appear when I open my hand, would you like to see it?" We all laughed, but he kept on, "No, really. I can make an elephant appear when I open my hand. I'll show you, but I have to be sure that you believe I can do it, first. Do you believe I can do it?"

SOMEONE
   "What, like a real elephant?" (laughter)

JOE
   "Yes, a real elephant." (more laughter. harder this time.)

SOMEONE(S)
   "Well, I'd like to see you try. Do it! Go ahead!"
   "Yeah! It's probably like a teeny little toy. Come on, let's see it!" (grumbles, murmurs, more laughter, but cynical this time.)

JOE
   "No, it's not a toy—it's a full-grown elephant, tusks and all, but it doesn't sound like you believe that I can actually do it, and I really need to know that you'll believe it, first, so . . . do you believe that I can do it?"

The noise of the room continued as before, but also began to escalate into the territory of confusion (and outright annoyance).

I was sitting towards the back and I don't really know how or why it happened, but I started to get this very weird prickly-goosebumpy vibe, and for the tiniest of moments I thought to myself, "Jeez, what if this is it? What if this is just like the moment in some superhero or sci-fi movie when something really unbelievable happens, and this guy, Joe, can actually produce a full grown elephant from the palm of his hand? What if this is the exact moment when everything I know about the world is completely overturned and something truly wild and impossible actually does happen? After all, it's just like that in the movies, right? The world is totally normal, and then, BAM! Everything changes and nothing is ever the same again! What if this is that moment, but for real!?"

I heard a clear and committed voice cry out above the noise of the room and I was probably more shocked than anyone when I realized that the voice was mine as I shouted,

"WOULD YOU SHUT UP AND LET HIM DO IT!?"

What happened next was truly extraordinary, and I'm not exaggerating one bit when I say that nothing has been the same for me ever since. Of course, the obvious question is, "So, what happened? Did he really produce a full-grown live elephant from the palm of his hand?" Well, I would love to tell you. I'd love to write it all down and shout it from the moon and put it on banners and billboards, but I can't stop from wondering if anyone would even believe it if they didn't see it for themselves, and so that's my problem. It's incredibly important to me, so I'd need to know that I'd be believed before I revealed what really occurred. I mean, come on, if I told you that some guy named Joe made a full-grown elephant appear from the palm of his hand, would you believe it?

047

An Email from a Very Old Ancestor

To: Humans (distribution list too large to expand)
From: A hundred-million-year-old lizard

Subject: Hey!

Hey!

So nice to talk to you like this—technology really
is something, right? I've been meaning to reach out
to you for a long time, but you know how it is: One day
you're eating a bug, and the next thing you know, several
million years have gone by. Well, anyway, the first thing
that I'd like you to know about me is that I have been very,
very anxious for a long, long time. A hundred million years
ago, other than wanting to eat and to make more of us, most
of the thoughts in my head were things like:

"GAH! DANGER! RUN!" or **"GAH! DANGER! ATTACK!"** or
"GAH! DANGER! SHHH! DON'T. MOVE. A. MUSCLE!"

I made it, though, and not everybody did. I remember seeing
all these laid-back lizards just hangin' out, not a care in the
world, and do you know where they are now?
They're **DEAD**, that's where!

Only the most nervous of us made it far enough to become
you, which has been no small feat, so, you know,
YOU'RE WELCOME!

I also developed this feature that these days, smart people
call a "negativity bias," but we didn't call it that back then.
Frankly, we didn't say much of anything, except maybe
"hsssss," or sometimes, "thhphhphthhp." At first glance, just
about everything I see seems like a threat to me. Sure,
it doesn't always feel great to see a predator behind **EVERY.
SINGLE. TREE**—but it's better to have a super-nervous walk

in the woods than a dead one, amiright? I mean, if I don't bag a bug for lunch today, then maybe I'll get one tomorrow, but screw up and not see that big thing with teeth eyeing me up? WHAMO! No more bugs for me forever!

So yeah, I'm pretty proud of my part in our story. I kept us safe, and hey, it's not my fault that your brains got bigger and bigger and you developed agriculture and cities and airplanes and stuff like that. It's not my fault that you carry all of my finely-tuned, jungle-tested survival instincts into classrooms, meetings, social media platforms, late nights staring at ceilings, traffic, lines at stores, family gatherings, doctors' offices, pool parties, job interviews, bars, and—well, you get the picture. It's funny to hear it, though. People feel anxious and nervous and stuff, and they wonder to themselves, "Why do I feel this way? Why am I so broken?" and I just lick my eyeball and shake my head and think,

Do you know how much went into this?
Do you have any idea how hard I had to work and how lucky I had to be?
Do you realize how many sharp teeth we avoided feeling this way?
Do you have any clue at all how long it took to make humans... **human?!**

LIKE, MILLIONS AND MILLIONS OF YEARS!!
(give or take a dozen billion)

Nooo, my future-me friend, you're not broken, far from it. All of that anxiety, worry, stress, guilt, regret, insecurity, embarrassment, depression, despair, anger, rage, frustration? You're operating exactly like a perfectly evolved, normal human being, even when it doesn't feel so good, so . . . **CONGRATS!**

Of course, that big brain of yours can do so much more these days—if you ask it to. Don't get me wrong, I'm pretty proud of how I kept us safe out there in the forests and jungles and grasslands and deserts, but maybe you don't have to feel that way to survive anymore. Maybe you could use that head of yours to choose another way of being, maybe something like love or joy or connection or whatever you want, but I did my part. What comes next is totally up to you.

Good luck!

Your friend,
thhphhphthhp

048 Let Life Live You

Every year, year after year, life asks that
    trees drop their leaves in the fall and create new ones
    in the spring,
    ruby-throated hummingbirds migrate from North
    America to Central America in the fall, and then return
    in the spring,
    humpback whales travel up to 5,000 miles from
    summer feeding grounds in the north to tropical waters
    in the south to calve,
    thousands upon thousands of wildebeests follow
    the rain along the same looped path during their
    annual migration.

Why do I think for a moment that I'm any different?
And yet I fight it.
    I lack and I want and I thirst and I crave and I run away
    and I run towards and I run against and I claw and
    I scratch and I regret and I damn and I hate and I try
    and I try and I try and
it all feels like trying to stop an ocean wave with my bare hands.

When I listen, though—when I really listen, I can hear life
telling me what it wants from me.

It says
    be patient
    and
    be helpful
    and
    be kind
    and
    you're ok.

It says
    You don't have a life, I have a you. Stop thinking
    you have to live life. Let me live you.

049 Maybe

Once upon a time, there lived a very wise farmer.

One day, his only horse fled from his field, over the hills, and off into the distance. The villagers all cried to the farmer, "Oh no! That is so horrible!"
To which the farmer replied, "Maybe."

The next day, the horse returned to the farmer, bringing seven healthy and strong wild horses along with him. Astonished, the villagers cried, "How wonderful! What great fortune!"
To which the farmer replied, "Maybe."

Some days later, as the farmer's only son was attempting to tame one of the wild horses, he was thrown from the saddle and badly broke his arm. The villagers cried, "How dreadful! That's so terrible that your son is hurt!"
To which the farmer replied, "Maybe."

The following day, soldiers arrived in the village to conscript every able-bodied young person for the coming war with the neighboring clan. Seeing the farmer's son with his badly broken arm, they passed his house by. When the villagers learned of this, they congratulated the farmer on his wonderful luck, saying, "What great luck and fortune!"
To which the farmer replied, "Maybe."

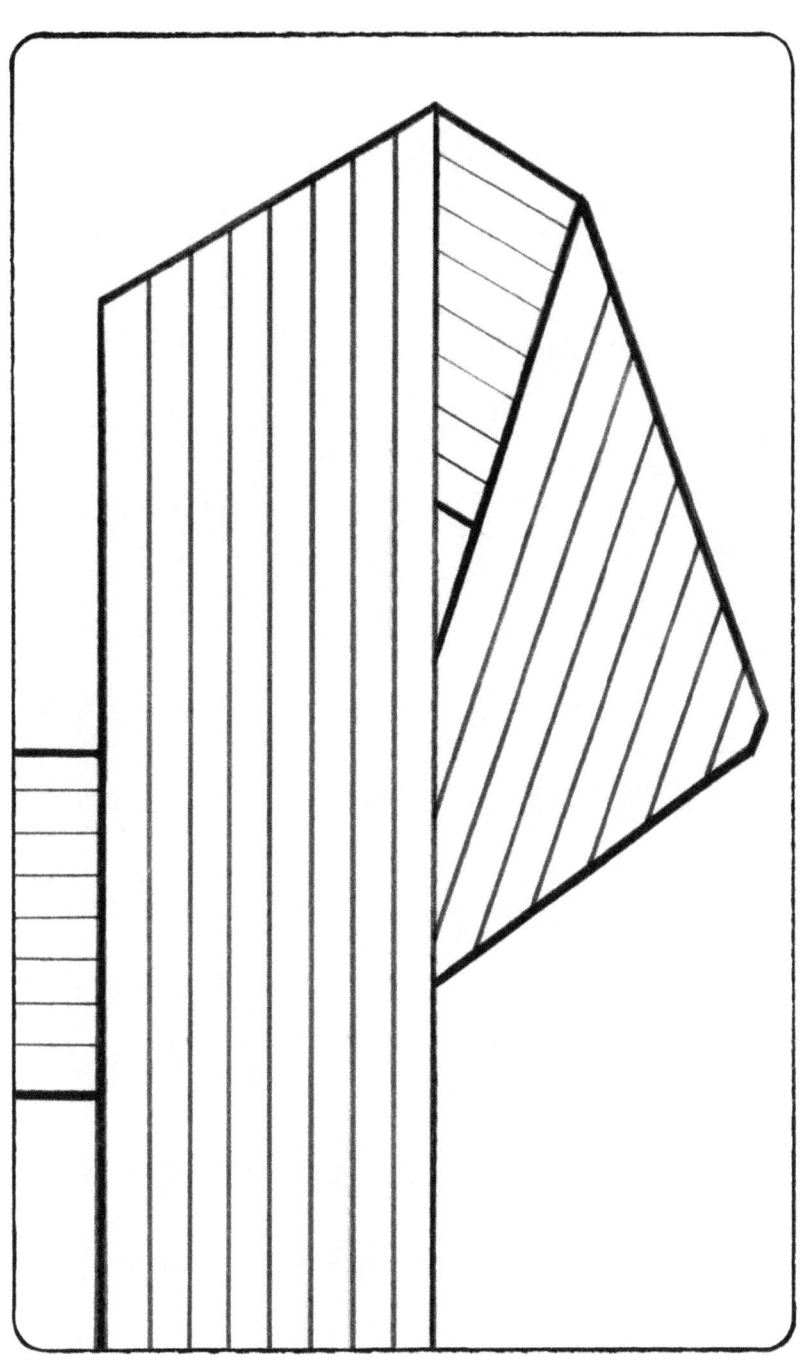

050 Herding Cats

I live with dozens of cats—maybe hundreds, I don't know.
I have no idea where they came from. I didn't adopt them
or buy them or rescue them, they just showed up (I can't even
remember when) and I can't get rid of them. When I try
to shoo the bad ones away, it only makes them meow
louder, and if I try to ignore them, even more seem
to appear.

I feel responsible for them. I'm not a "cat person," but they
all have such funny little faces and such silly little voices
that I can't help but look out for them. Dare I say I love them
(even though some of them really seem to want to cause
trouble). I've found that the trick to living with them is to keep
an eye out for them and care for them when they come
around, no matter what. If I do this, then they just sort
of saunter off, taking their own sweet time.

The one I named Good is so good, though. She is so gentle
and sweet. She never stays long enough, and she can be hard
to find, but she is so sweet. Between her, Giddy, Relaxed, and
Happy (I think they must be siblings), I could spend all day
with them.

Guilt, on the other hand, is a real pain. He clings to my leg
and yowls very loudly (too loudly). Although not as loudly
as the big Maine Coon, Regret. Man, Regret caterwauls
so raucously that he wakes me up (and then keeps me up).
I think he does it on purpose.

The twins, Insecure and Angry, drive me a little nuts. Every
time I try to feed Insecure, Angry jumps in front and hisses
at me, scaring Insecure half to death and making her run
away. I have no idea how she eats. I think maybe Angry
feeds her—the way they tend to be together, it's almost
as though Angry is just trying to keep Insecure safe.

The ones who make my heart truly ache, however, are Depressed, Lonely, and Despairing. They refuse to eat and don't seem to notice how much I pet them or tell them how pretty they are. They just stare, but not at anything that I can see. I've tried jingly toys and catnip and laser pointers, but they remain blank. I love them so much, though, and if I'm being honest, I think way down deep, they know it. I certainly hope they do.

I love them all, even though they're not really mine. Cats are like that, I guess. They come and they go and none of them seem to particularly give a hoot about me, but I care for them anyway. Like I said, the trick is to notice them when they're around, so my days are spent keeping my eyes peeled for when they show up so that I can make sure they have saucers of milk and big plates of tuna. I do my very best to make sure they know that I love them, no matter what. What else can I do? After all, they make my life exactly what it is, so how can I be anything but grateful?

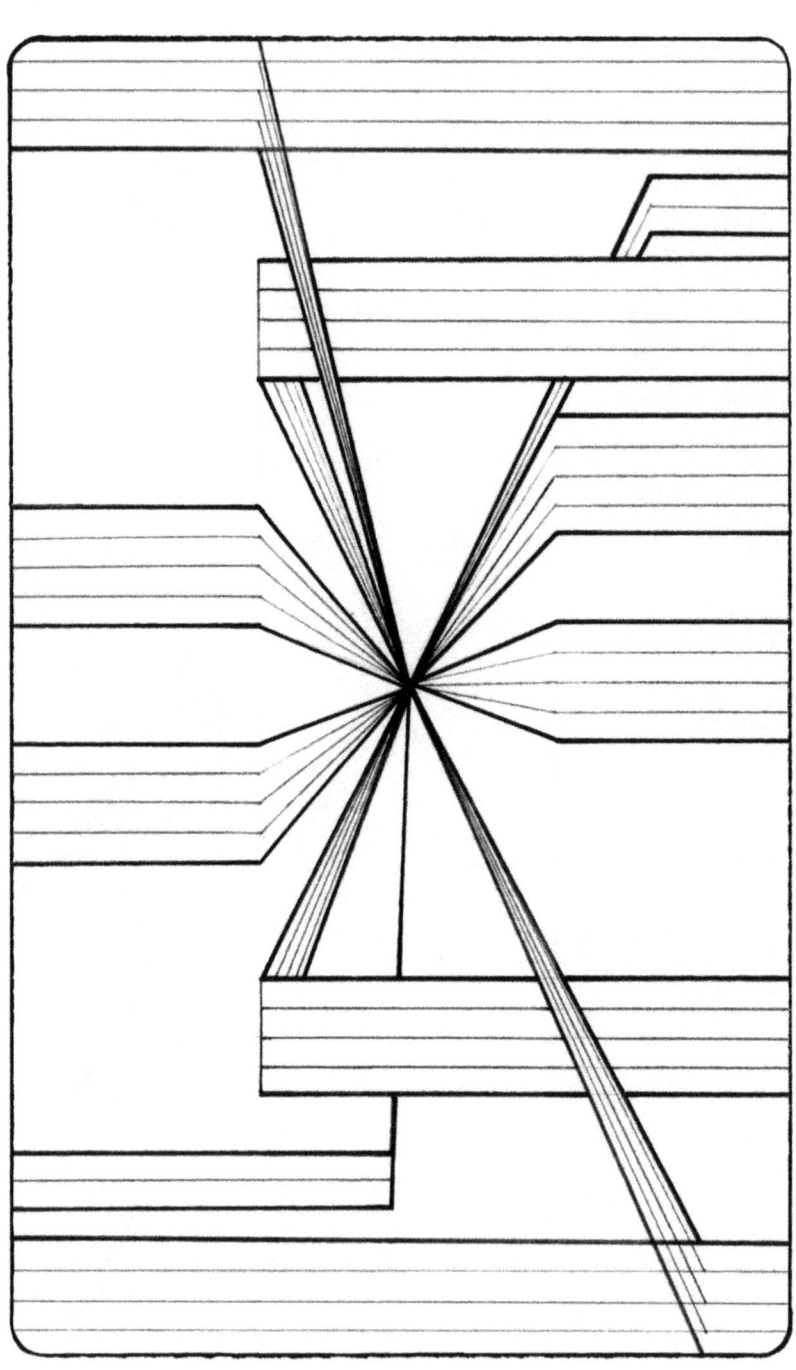

Past & Future Lives

I sometimes talk to the me at 12 or 17
or 27
or 80
or whenever I get the feeling now that they need me then.

I tell them things work out.
Things get interesting.
Things get low, but you don't end there.
Things never stop being beautiful.
Things that you said and did and regret and cringe about and
wish never happened
are OK—
are part of the wild weaving that led to now and
to all the incredible stuff that you hold most dear —
are part of the story of today.
You don't have to lose sleep over them.

I tell them that they're loved.

I tell them that they're OK.

I know they hear me,

and I hope they know just how grateful I am for them.

052 Oneness Is Not Sameness

In Oneness,
I am,
just as you are,
just as all things are,
but Oneness is not sameness.

Oneness shows itself through me, through you;
through an oak tree, or a cat, or an insect, or a stream,
or a star light years away.

I witness my being through my joys, just as I witness
it through my suffering.
I play and I dance,
just as I weep and grieve—
just as you do,
or an oak tree does,
or a cat,
or an insect,
or a stream,
or a star light years away.

Each with its own view.
Each shaped by its own
experience, place, and time.
Each performing what life
asks of it.
Each infinitely inventive.
Each a million billion experiments
of what's possible.

Each an expression of connection and interaction.

Each subject to the forces acted upon it and the impacts
of its actions—
its karma.

Each contributing to the delusion of separation.

Each resonating through one singular and undying voice: infinitely powerful, despite being most often only a whisper in the wind.

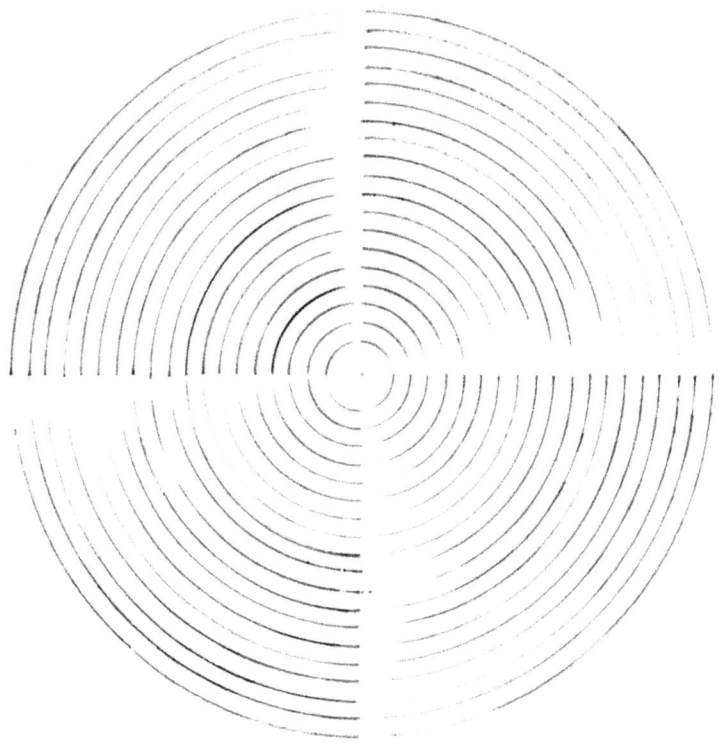

Thanking the Poisons

Thank you, Hatred.
Thank you for my need to be right and my need to defend.
You helped me try to make sense of the world through the
barriers you built. You provided people and ideas for me
to oppose in order to reinforce my own sense of security.
You created conflict, stress, and suffering, all in the name
of trying to somehow make me feel emboldened as I stood
alone against the world.

Hatred, please accept my thanks,
as well as my compassion, love, kindness, forgiveness,
and patience. May you not feel so alone and angry. May
you not need to defend yourself. May you not need
to defend anything.

Thank you, Greed.
Thank you for my unquenchable thirst and insecurity.
You gave me comparisons to others who I aspired to be
like. You helped me to find pleasure in what I knew would
be temporary. You created anxiety, a sense of lack, and
suffering, but I know that you were only trying to help
me fill the gap between who I thought I was and who
I thought I needed to be.

Greed, please accept my thanks,
as well as my generosity, selflessness, and gratitude. May
you come to know all that you already always are.

Thank you, Delusion.
Thank you for painting pictures of perfection and images
of separation between myself and all things. Thank you
for being the father and mother to both my Hatred and
my Greed, for making me think that I needed them
in order to build a happy life. Thank you for my feelings
of being both better-than and worse-than, lucky and
unlucky, fortunate and unfortunate.

Delusion, please accept my thanks,
as well as my wisdom, clarity, and mindful insight. May you
see the world as it truly is, and take refuge in what is whole.

Dear Poisons,
Thank you for looking out for me when I didn't know where
else to turn. I've known each of you for as long as I can
remember. We literally grew up together, and I can't thank
you enough for bringing me here to this place right here and
now. It was only through you that I discovered that
we no longer have to suffer, that we can be free.

Thank you,
but you can sit down now and rest. I'll take it from here.

054　Crash Course

It was an absolutely beautiful day, so I thought I'd take the kayak out into the lake. As I was paddling around, enjoying the day and the breeze, feeling happy to be alive, I noticed another boat heading my way. This boat wasn't just headed in my general direction, though. This sucker was coming straight at me, so I sat-up and shouted,

Hey!

. . . but nothing happened, so I shouted a little louder,

Hey! You're heading right for me!

. . . but the oncoming boat didn't change course at all. Not one bit, so I started to get really annoyed, and I thought to myself,

What is this idiot doing?
What's wrong with this freakin' guy?

. . . but the boat was still coming. In fact, it was going to ram right into me!

DUDE!!
YOU'RE GOING TO RAM RIGHT INTO ME!!

. . . but still no change! At this point, I started to really freak out, like, really **FOR-REAL** freak out,

YOU IDIOT!!!
WHAT IS WRONG WITH YOU?!?!
WHAT ARE YOU DOING?!?!?

I started to paddle like crazy to get out of the way, and darned if I didn't miss that other boat by mere inches. You can imagine how hard I craned my neck around to get a good look at that stupid, careless, no good, ignorant sonofagun.

You can also imagine my surprise when I discovered that the boat was empty.

055　Enlightenment in a Canoe

My buddy, Kris, started goofing around with woodworking
maybe a year ago—making cutting boards, then chess
boards, then a really cool bookshelf for his daughter, but
then . . . a canoe!

A CANOE.

Our friend Gernot and I asked him how he did it. We both
went on and on about how amazed we were about the whole
thing: how beautiful it turned out and how much fun it was
to live through its construction over months and months
of our group texts. We also told him how amazed we were
that he had the courage to even attempt it. I told him that
it felt like someone taking up the piano and then learning
Rachmaninoff's 2nd Concerto to perform with the Chicago
Symphony, all in a few months.

Kris laughed and said that his wife, Iva, had a lot to do with
it. She lent him her office in their apartment in Vienna
so he could store tons of wood and a bunch of really loud
woodworking equipment—which she was happy to do.

He also said that it was about having patience and about
"surrendering to the little processes." He said it was about
being OK with whatever step he was in while he was in it.

He said it wasn't really about making a canoe as much
as it was about . . . sanding,
and sanding,
and sanding,
followed by applying some lacquer,
and then
more sanding.

He said it was more about being in those moments than
it was about "making a canoe."

He said that the canoe just kind of happened.

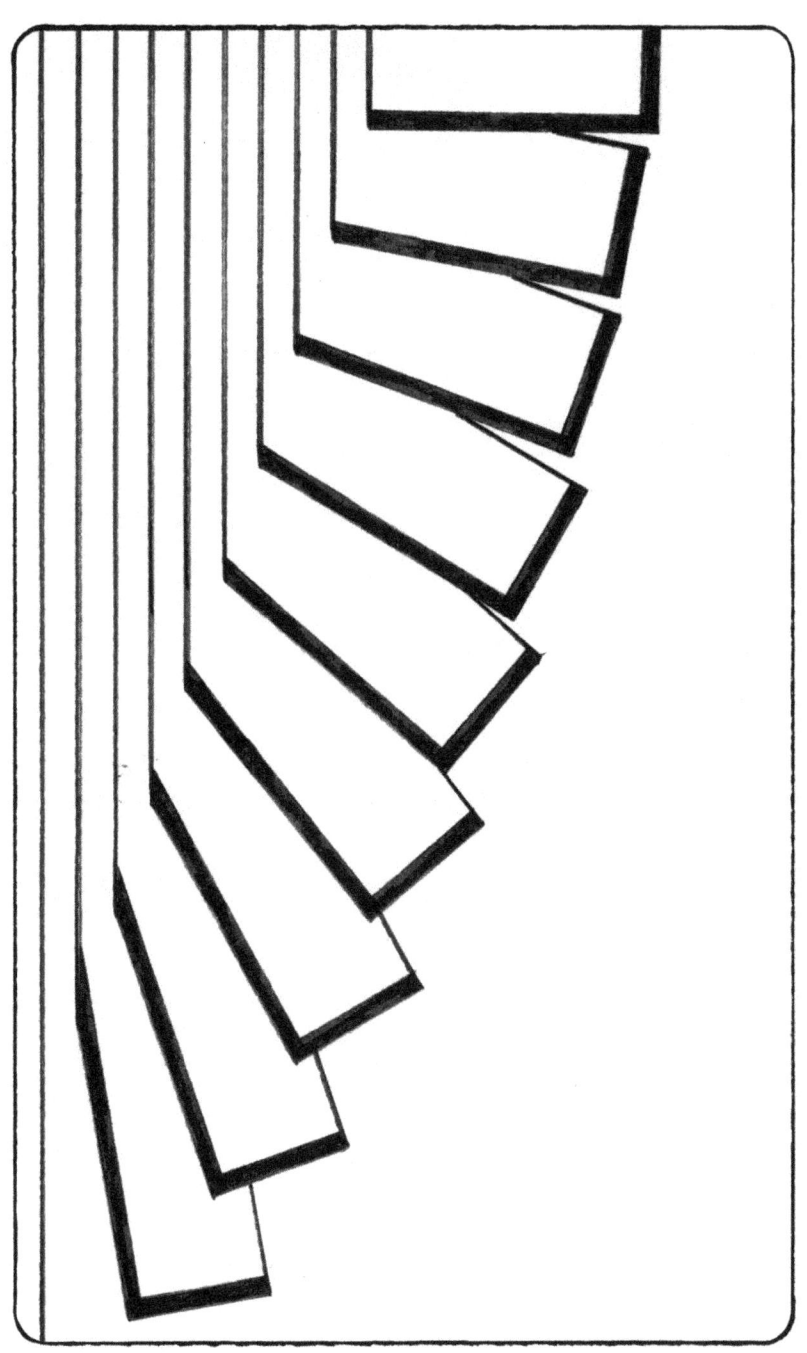

I lost my very first "real" job out of college before it even
started. A product that the company had released earlier
that year had not performed well, so instead of moving
to Boston, I moved back in with my parents. Instead
of living some new awesome life, I found myself sleeping
in my old bedroom and working a very uncool job:

Do Until DEMORALIZED = 100%
> Hi, this is Mike calling with (insert name of horrible
> company), this call may be monitored for quality. May
> I speak to the person responsible for the telephone
> account? Oh! Oh no! I'm sorry! I'm so sorry! I'll put
> you on our do-not-call list immediately!

Repeat

Looking at it now, none of my circumstances were even
remotely that bad, certainly nowhere nearly as bad
as many folks endure every day, nor even as bad as what
I've come to experience myself since then, but my story
about them was that bad, and unfortunately this is all
that ever really matters. Such is the power of our stories:
They drive everything.

I remember this being the first "dark period" I'd faced
as a new adult. I remember, for the first time, finding
myself surrounded by black walls that I couldn't see over.
I remember feeling trapped. I remember feeling like I had
no control over my own life, and that there was a real
possibility that I never would. I remember motionless
depression and vibrating anxiety. I remember wishing
I could do anything to make it change or go away.

I don't wish that kind of period on anyone, and yet
I find myself deeply grateful for it now. Had it not been for
that terrible job, then I would not have met my wife (who
worked there, as well), which means we would not have
our wonderful child, or our dogs, or the millions

of laughs, or the countless moments of support, or anything that glows brightest in my chest today.

With very little effort, I can trace everything I hold most dear to me directly back to that period of time, knowing that the most wonderful moments today needed the difficult ones as chapters in their story, or verses in their song.

I take great refuge in this as I face other difficult times, knowing that difficult times are always the birthplace for something not-yet-known, but inevitably wonderful.

057 Perfecting

Within the dharma, there are six Perfections, or Paramitas:

> Generosity, known as Dana
> Virtue, known as Sila
> Patience, known as Kshanti
> Energy, known as Virya
> Focus, known as Dhyana
> Wisdom, known as Prajna

Para means "the other shore," or "enlightenment,"
and Mita means "measured."
In this way, Paramita means
the state of one who is fully awakened or enlightened.

But as enlightenment is a state of being
And being is a state of flowing
And flowing is a state
of effortless movement within change,
then the Perfections
are not about being perfect.

After all, "perfect" is static, defined, and contained, and how
could enlightenment be contained?

The Perfections are forever moving—

Forever growing

Forever screwing it up, but then making it right
Forever straying, but then coming back
Forever stagnating, but then stepping forward
Forever placing fingers on wrong keys, until one day: music

Forever expanding outward
Forever traveling inward

Forever dissolving the boundaries between myself and other
Forever realizing what's already there

Forever perfecting

058

Generosity (*Dana*)

Perfecting generosity is coming to know that I'm always
overflowing, and so always free to give.

I've hidden the ads multiple times at this point, but social
media keeps presenting the most heartbreaking images
of dogs in cages to me, asking me to save them by donating,
and I have donated, time and time again, and yet I can't
keep up. I'll never keep up. It seems like my donations
aren't making a dent. The images stick with me, though,
their eyes go right through me. Why do I give at all? How
can I possibly make any difference? And it doesn't end here!
How can I hope to even make a dent to stop climate change,
or poverty, or wars, or deforestation, or children's cancer?

> I can't.
> My actions alone are likely not nearly enough,
> but my actions are what I have,
> and so. . .

I can give my ears to listen to a friend whose desperate
thoughts are swimming and they just need to be heard.

I can encounter those who disagree with me, knowing that
they only want exactly what I want: to be free, to feel peace,
to love and be loved.

I can reach out to someone who is lonely.

I can pick up the dead bird in the street so the neighbor's
tiny girl doesn't see it from her Big Wheel.

I can help those closest to me without any expectation
of return.

I can donate to the Humane Society or the ASPCA
or St. Jude's or wherever whenever I am able and inspired
to do so.

I can pray. I can set my intent. I can reflect.

I can do all of these things (and more) the smallest amount
better today than I did yesterday, and I can commit to doing
them better tomorrow, even when I fail.

059

Virtue (*Sila*)

Perfecting morality is hearing the voice of my awakened heart more clearly than the judgment of my mind.

Imagine a circle that represents any given moral question:

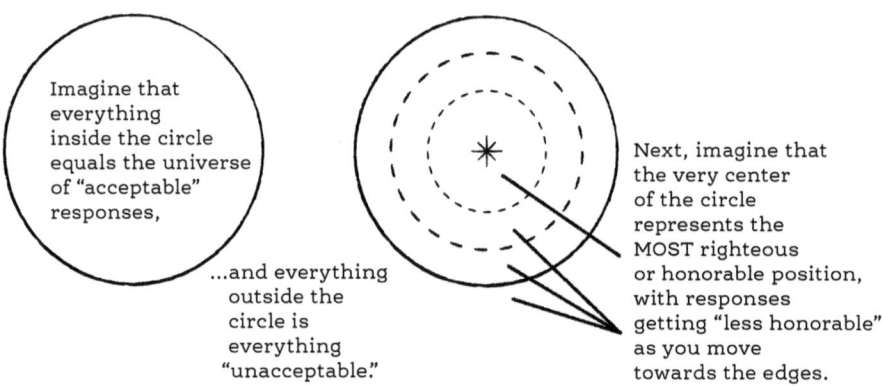

Imagine that everything inside the circle equals the universe of "acceptable" responses,

...and everything outside the circle is everything "unacceptable."

Next, imagine that the very center of the circle represents the MOST righteous or honorable position, with responses getting "less honorable" as you move towards the edges.

For example, in most work settings, a manager saying, "You look really nice today," is likely OK (that is, it would fall within the circle), but it isn't the MOST NOBLE ACTION. The most noble action is probably not to comment on anyone's appearance at work, but rather to keep compliments to things like doing a great job, making an incredible effort, demonstrating resilience in the face of challenges, etc.

Everything I do has an impact. This is known as karma. Every single one of my actions influences the universe in some way. Knowing this, I also know that the moral position I take, no matter where it resides within the circle, can become a reference point for someone else's moral circle—in fact, it's possible that it could become the center of their circle!

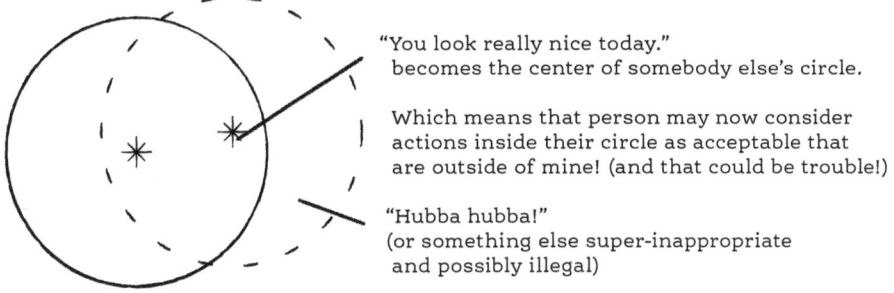

"You look really nice today."
becomes the center of somebody else's circle.

Which means that person may now consider actions inside their circle as acceptable that are outside of mine! (and that could be trouble!)

"Hubba hubba!"
(or something else super-inappropriate and possibly illegal)

Stay as close as possible to the very center of the circle!

060 Patience (*Kshanti*)

Perfecting patience is being precisely and fully here,
wherever that may be.

Patience can sometimes disguise itself as passive, like a kind
of tortuous lack of control where I'm forced to be okay with
something happening "to me" that I cannot stop, change,
or escape.

Looking more closely, though, patience is anything but
passive. What could take more iron resolve than wanting
desperately for something to be different, but knowing that
it isn't imminently possible, and sitting with it anyway? What
could take more discipline and focus than to sit in the fires
of emotion with only the wisdom in my heart?

Breathing in
I see the flames of my wanting clearly, no matter how they
bang in my skull
or dance in my stomach.
I know that I am not at my wanting's beck and call.
I know that I am not my wanting's prisoner.
I know that I am not owned or defined by my wanting.
I know that the fire of my wanting needs my oxygen.
I know that it is within me to fan it further,
or to starve it.

Breathing out
I know that, at this moment, I am whole
    —just as I am.

I know that, at this moment, all is complete
    —exactly as it is.

I know that, at this moment, everything is precisely as life
asks it to be
    —nothing to be added; nothing to be subtracted.

I blow out the inferno like a candle flame.

061 Energy & Perseverance (*Virya*)

Perfecting energy is watching a leaf ride the shoulders of a stream and knowing that I, too, am that.

I don't recall Todd ever missing a sunrise. He'd set his alarm based on it, and even on days that were cloudy or threatening to storm, he'd send me pictures of the dim sky and sea becoming radiant and bright. No matter what the day delivered afterward, he made a point of ensuring that it started with this special transmission beyond words or scriptures.

The path to the sacred is not only one that I walk upon, but one that I build as I go. I lay the very bricks upon which I tread. I create my own awakening.

But how should I practice? Which practice is best? Do I meditate? Do I chant? If so, for how long? What if I think chanting is ridiculous? Do I read? If so, what do I read? Do I join a monastery? Do I shave my head? If I don't shave my head, am I not doing it right? Can I eat burgers? Can I have a beer? What if it's a really good beer?

The best practice I can do is the one that I WILL do.

Practice does not need to be marathon meditation sessions on mountain tops, it only needs to move me forward, no matter how big or small that movement might be.

The practice that I do is the one I'm called to do in my heart:

A daily prayer, intention, or meditation, no matter how long.

A walk around the neighborhood, noticing anything
and everything that calls to me as beautiful.

A cup of coffee with three conscious breaths
and a reminder of all the people and things that had
to happen for that coffee to exist in that mug in my hand.

A new day shared with a sunrise not taken for granted.

Focus (*Dhyana*)

Perfecting concentration is this very moment noticed.

It's not about "not having any thoughts" or "emptying the mind." It's about beginning again:

The Magic is in beginning again, like stringing beads on a mala.

I point my attention to my shoulders.
I watch them and feel them
and let them relax.

I notice that my attention has left my shoulders and I know that it's ok.

I point my attention to my breath.
I watch it and feel it and
find myself as one with it.

I notice that my attention has left my breath and I'm fine with it. It's just my brain doing what brains do: squirrels squirrel, trees tree, and brains brain.

I point my attention to the sounds around me: the birds, the traffic, the hum of the air conditioner.
I hear them and feel them and find myself as one with them.

I notice that my attention has left the sounds around me and I know it's perfectly normal and good.

I point my attention to my energy flowing within me: the subtle hum of life singing to me from within.
I sense it and feel it and find myself as one with it.

I notice that my attention has left the energy flowing within me and I'm perfectly cool with it.

I point my attention to my breath, to the sounds around me, to the force of life within me, to whatever I choose. I watch them and feel them and find myself as one with them.

I notice that my attention has departed. My mind has shifted to something perfectly human: a worry, an itch, a song from the 1980s. I not only allow it, but I am friends with it. I am grateful for the moments of attention, no matter how brief, and know that I can return to them whenever I choose.

063 Wisdom (*Prajna*)

Perfecting wisdom is awakening to the reality that nothing exists in and of itself, that nothing is unchanging and alone.

———————————————

All that there is
is one vast song.
Every note and every rest
is a shoulder upon which the other lays its head.

Sound is
because silence is,
and silence is
because sound is.

Listen!

Listen like someone you love is whispering a secret from across the room.

Listen!

064 Float

The sea is so rough and
It's all darkness and gray and
The waves are too high and
My feet can't touch and
I can't see the shore—
I can't see anything but water and
I can't tread water anymore and
I'm drowning—I feel it—I'm drowning and
It's too much and

I stop and
I spread my arms and legs outward and
I lean back and
I remember that
I float!
I breathe and
I float!
I see stars!
So many stars!
And I'm carried
By the sea and the sky—
And I float!

Feeling Is an Open Door

For just a few moments,
forget words, or at least forget the need to find them.

There are so many problems to chew through,
but choose to set them aside.
Worries will wait—no need to worry about that.

Feel my head and imagine a crown of grace
and wisdom atop it.
Feel my eyelids and let them rest.
Feel my ears and let them droop.
Feel my tongue and let it slacken.
Feel my jaw and let it slouch.
Feel my shoulders and let them
let go of their burdens.
Feel my elbows and let gravity hug them.
Feel my hands and let them sparkle.
Feel my chest and let it pulse.
Feel my stomach and let it sleepily yawn.
Feel my hips and let them thaw.
Feel my legs and let them warm.
Feel my calves and let them glow.
Feel my feet and let them shimmer.
Feel everything I am at once:

A light lit from within,
A pulsing beacon,
A sun,
A source,
A sonata.

A question that's content to remain open.
Unanswered and yet somehow surefooted.

Myself and yet somehow more.

066   What Happens When You Die?

Some say that when you die you go to heaven, but only
if you've earned it. Some say you go to hell. Some say nothing
happens at all, you just die. You just end. Just blackness—
vast, endless, terrifying blackness for all of eternity.
Some say it's not blackness or anything terrifying, just . . .
nothing, the same exact nothing that you didn't experience
before you were born.

Do you remember what it was like before you were born?
Well, they say it's like that.

Some of the answers sound really good to me.
Some of them scare me.
Some of them puzzle me.

I like the idea of hanging out in some beautiful place (like a really
nice beach) with everyone I've ever known and loved (and maybe
a whole bunch of people I haven't met yet), but . . . forever?

Forever ever?
Forever ever ever?
Forever ever ever ever ever ever ever ever ever ever . . . ?

When it comes right down to it, though, I have to wonder why
I'm asking the question in the first place.

Why do I need to know?

Or maybe more to the point:
Who wants to know? I mean, really . . .

Who is it that's asking?

I guess that's my problem with the whole thing. All the
opinions seem to assume a very clear and definite answer
as to who the "you" is in the question, and I'm just not
sure I'm able to put my finger on that yet.

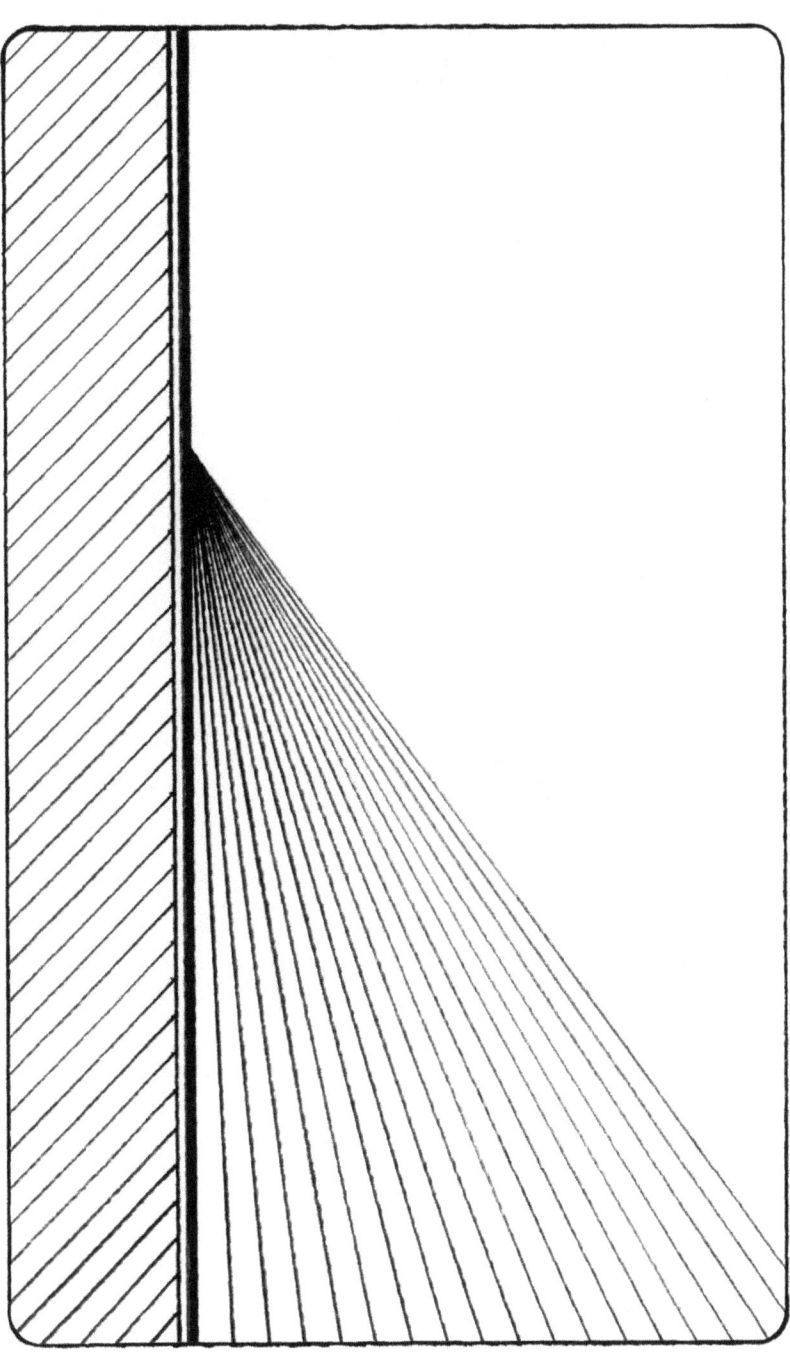

067

Pulling the Rug Out from Under Myself

I am my body, right? I'm my "stuff": my arms and hair and
stomach and brain and heart and every weird little gland
thing that does something I have no clue about, but that
stuff is me, right?

> . . . but which stuff? The stuff today? I know I'm me, and
> I remember being me when I was a kid, but goodness
> knows that 13-year-old me and 25-year-old me and
> 50-year-old me look very different. Is there stuff
> that's the same? I understand that except for some
> cells in my eyes, everything else is totally replaced
> every seven to fifteen years, so none of the 13-year-
> old me "stuff" even remains at all. Heck, that makes
> me "me v4.0" at this point—
> so who am I?

Maybe I'm my feelings. I have strong emotions that are
wholly mine. When I feel joy, that's me. When I feel profound
sadness, that's me, too. I'm definitely those feelings, right?

> . . . but those come and go like the wind. One moment
> I can feel one way, and then be completely taken
> to another place. My feelings are totally transient,
> so who am I?

Maybe I'm how I perceive the world: the things I like, the
things I don't like, and the things I don't care about at all.
Maybe these are what make me unique and make me . . .
"me," right?

> . . . but just like my stuff and my feelings, my perceptions
> also change. Sure, I wanted to be Eddie Van Halen in the
> worst way when I was 16, but now? Not as much—
> so who am I?

Maybe I'm how I view myself in the world and my will
to accomplish things. I know the kinds of people I want
to be around, I know my work, I know where I fit in compared
to everybody else, and I know what I want to do.

> . . . but again, this stuff has changed countless times,
> there's no way to put my finger on it—
> so who am I?

Maybe I'm all of them, combined. When one changes, they all
change. To boot, I'm the ground on which all of them play:
my consciousness, and all of this swirling together is my real
identity. Maybe I can confidently say that this is me: I look
like this, I feel this way, I like this stuff, I do these things
. . . this is who I am!

> . . . but all of this changes, too. It's always changing,
> there is nothing permanent about any of it, not one
> thing. Who am I? It's all a big crazy moving target, and
> it could really drive me crazy (and make me more than
> a little scared) if I let it.

Thankfully, though, when I look out my window,
when I really look,
when I let it in,
when I touch the stillness of it—the is-ness—
when I'm with it so much
that I can't really distinguish myself apart from it whatsoever,

then something new appears
and I find myself not really needing to ask much
of anything at all.

068

Judgment

Sometimes, when I see someone driving like an absolute maniac, swerving around cars in the right-hand lane, going at breakneck speeds, flooring it through heavy traffic and endangering everyone else on the whole highway, I like to say to myself, "Wow, that person must really have to pee."
—Anonymous

I watched a friend of mine play the role of "jerk" perfectly. They responded to a National Public Radio social media post with a comment that was so insensitive and hurtful that I had to blink my eyes a few times to be sure that it was coming from their username. Not at all surprisingly, their comment received all of the rights and privileges worthy of a "jerk" job well-done: dozens of replies both decrying what they wrote and wondering why they wrote it at all. Why be so hurtful? Why be so mean? What are they getting out of it?

Again, this person is a friend of mine. I know them well and like them very much. I know them to be a good person with a good heart, so I was as dumbfounded as I was disgusted. Little did they know that their comment hit close to home and felt hurtful to me, personally, so I did the single cruelest thing that I have power to do—I passed right by anger and went directly to the maximum sentence available to me: apathy. I wrote them off. I erased them from my mind, deciding they were now someone I would no longer care about at all. Declaring, "I'm done with you," I banged the gavel in my mind and I unfollowed them from the platform.

A couple of days later, this person posted on another platform (that I forgot to unfriend them from). It was a picture of their super-beloved dog who had passed away a few months earlier next to a picture of a very sweet-faced Labrador Retriever that they had been fostering. The caption read that they learned two days ago that the lab was diagnosed with the same disease that took their best furry-headed friend in the world from them, and that they were about to live through the same nightmare again. Everything suddenly looked very different to me, and I couldn't help but feel my heart open again.

069 Rock-Bottomless

Of all the great temples and sacred places on this earth, some of the most holy and powerful can be found in church basements, community centers, and anywhere where addiction and recovery groups congregate.

They are true realms of living Bodhisattvas—
people with the experience of having stared directly into the devil's horrible red eyes, having brought with them to that battle every last crumb of self-worth, willpower, and heart, every last measure of who they remember they are, every last breath of hope,

only to lose.

Again.

Only to find that they haven't yet found rock-bottom, and in that discovery, come to realize that they may not have one—certainly not one that they're likely to find alive.

And yet they fight on,

in a circle of plastic chairs alongside people just like everyone and also not like anyone, all flirting with the blinding reality that they may be rock-bottomless.

And in their rock-bottomless-ness,
their eyes shine and ears bend with an understanding that is completely, totally, and utterly devoid of judgment.

To sit with them is to sit in the presence of the stark-naked human heart, one whose sorrows may have depths which may never be known, but whose compassion is as limitless as the sky.

070 Milarepa's Guests

Once upon a long time ago in a quiet Himalayan cave, there lived a mystic named Milarepa. Living in a cave may sound unpleasant to some, but to Milarepa, it was home. He had a simple robe to keep him warm, a pot in which to boil water, and plenty of nettles that he gathered from the hillsides to eat. Indeed, it is said that Milarepa ate so many nettles that his skin turned green! Pleasantly alone in his cave, Milarepa studied the Dharma, meditated, and reflected. He recited sutras, practiced yoga, and tended to the generous fire in his simple hearth, and in his peaceful heart.

One day, after a brief journey to collect firewood, Milarepa returned to his home only to find a most shocking and unwelcome sight—demons! Everywhere, demons: large and small, terrifying and ridiculous, fanged and clawed, hoofed and winged. Milarepa's home was overrun!

"Get out! Away with you! Shoo!" Milarepa cried, flapping his arms and stomping about, but the demons only laughed at him. Milarepa jumped and twirled and cried out, "Leave! You are not welcome here! Begone!" but the demons only laughed harder. Exhausted and exasperated, Milarepa was suddenly struck with great inspiration: He would teach them the Dharma of the Buddha! Sitting in the very center of his cave, he raised a finger in the air and began to recite, "Thus have I heard!" only to be met with expressionless, bored, and drooling faces from each and every creature around him.

With a deep breath and resignation to his new fate, Milarepa laid himself down to rest and sighed, "Well, I guess we will all just live together, then," and at that—POOF!—the demons disappeared! The cacophony of their cackles and gurgles was gone in an instant, and Milarepa was relieved to find himself once again surrounded by only the gentle crackling of his fire.

But something deep within Milarepa told him that he was mistaken. Lurking in the furthest and darkest corner of his cave, one demon remained. It was huge and terrible: the breath from its gaping mouth a putrid steam, its teeth an icy saw, its matted fur a cloak of despair and terror. With great courage, Milarepa approached the demon, looked directly into the void of its empty eyes, and said, "I see you, but I will not leave, and you cannot chase me away." Milarepa then placed his head directly into the mouth of the beast, for he knew deeply that to be devoured by any demon was his decision alone—that even with its teeth upon his neck, the demon was powerless without Milarepa's consent. Milarepa looked around from inside its cavernous jaws and noticed the glow of the fire reflecting from the demon's jagged and broken teeth, and he exclaimed, "What wondrous jewels here! What beauty!" And at that the demon backed away from Milarepa, placed its clawed hands together in front of its chest, bowed deeply, and vanished into the air.

Icons, Not Idols

Behold!
The Venerable One!
The World-Honored One!
The Enlightened One!
The Awakened One!
The Gone Thus Forth!
The Tathagata!
The Buddha!
Bow!
Gassho!
Prostrate!
On your knees!
On your belly!
Shake with wonder and humility!
Look upon this face,
this golden body,
this perfect composure,
this perfect knowing,
this perfect wisdom,
this perfect compassion,
this perfect peace emanating outward to all horizons,
to all worlds,
to everything there ever was,
is,
and will be!
Look!
Look and recognize this luminous being, but . . .

Do not pray to it!
Do not worship it!
No!
See it true!
See it as it is!

That's not a statue of stone, resin, or wood,
Not something carved in mountains,
Nor towering hundreds of feet into the sky,
Nor seated on holy altars,
Nor drawn with delicate, careful lines.

No, what you see is a mirror—
one that may just need a little polishing.
What you see is you.

072 Thought Experiment

Picture yourself in the very last moments of your life. Your physical death is imminent and upon you, but here's the thing: You have absolutely no fear or sadness or anything even remotely resembling them. In fact, it's just the opposite, you find yourself almost overwhelmed with feelings of peace, love, and gratitude. You're surrounded by people who love you and who you love fully. You feel complete. You feel whole. You feel wonderfully and absolutely blessed.

The thought experiment, then, is:

Why? Between now and that moment, what happened?

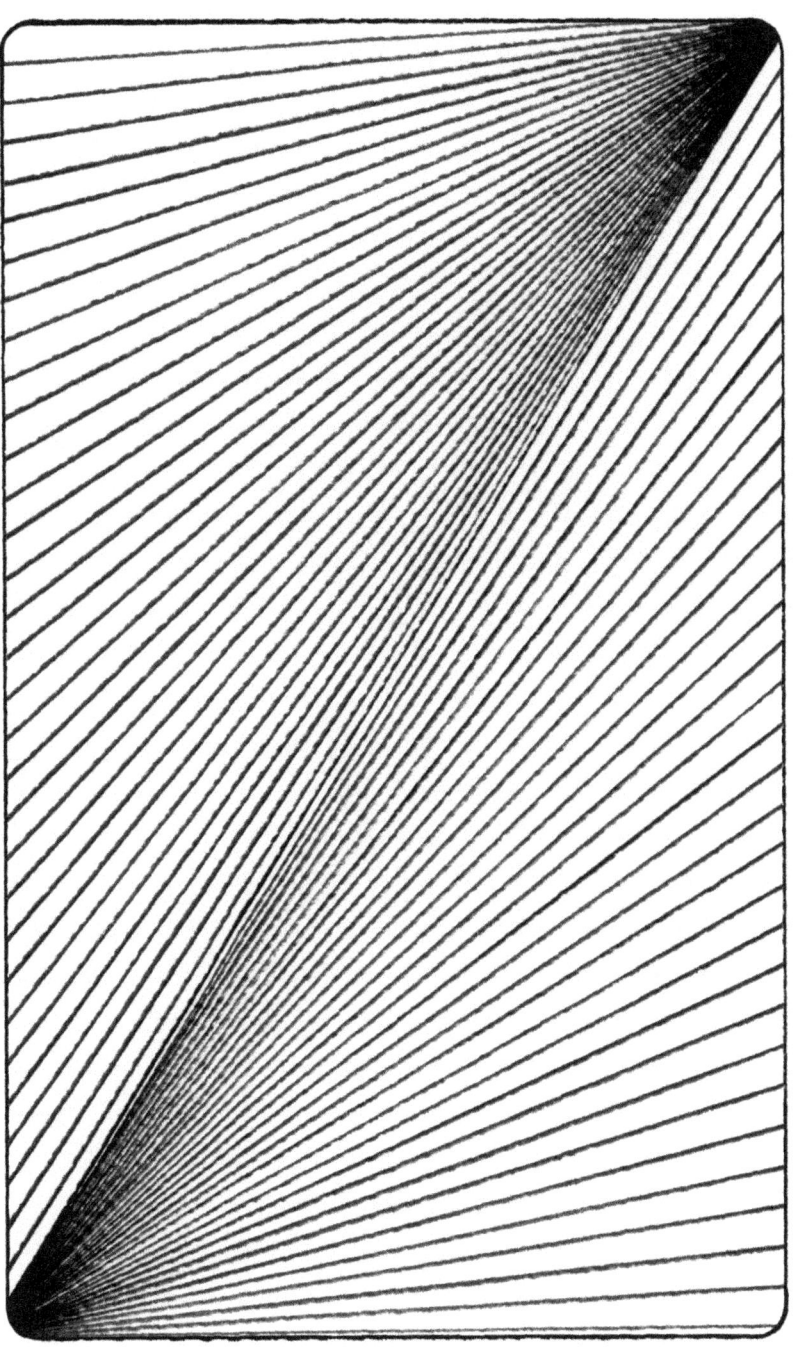

073 Weighing What Matters

If I'm fortunate enough to know that my time in this human
life is near its end, I wonder how I'll measure it.

Will I reflect on everything that I've accomplished?
    All the apartments and houses I lived in,
    All the cars I traded for other cars,
    All the social media followers and likes and reshares,
    All the places I wandered and loved or tried to escape,
    All the jobs and positions I left or started
    or lost or wanted,
    All the relationships I acquired, cultivated, or eroded,
    All the art I let in or blocked out with
    disgust or annoyance,
    All the people I helped to shape, or whose light made mine
    brighter or dimmer.

Will these things matter to me, or will I wonder, as so many
have before in that quiet coda:
    Was I trustworthy?
    Was I truthful?
    Was I able to forgive and allow myself to be forgiven?
    Was I able to love unconditionally?
    Was I able to recognize and account for any harm for which
    I was responsible?
    Was I able to understand the true wealth of character?
    Was I able to honor the precious rarity that is being here?
    Was I able to do everything possible to help the people
    I love feel in their very bones just how much I love them?
    Was I helpful?

As I read this now,
    may I remember that I build the answers to those
    questions by what I do now and next, and may I arrive
    in those final moments without any doubts.

Origin Story

In the beginning, God said,

Let there be light!

and you were born.

From the end of some unsaid sentence,
You boomed out of the darkness.
An unheard roaring light of everything that there will ever be,
Expanding and exploring, experimenting—
    A music,
    Scored as vast nebulae
    And crescendos of starlight.
Cooling and twirling, becoming—
    A ballet,
    Costumed as stone and sea,
    And leaping firebirds of life.
    Moving and masquerading,
    Dancing and dreaming.
Eons of new moments implied by their ancestors—
    Every effect having a cause,
    Every because having a why,
    Every singular point a snapshot of one uninterrupted
    drama arriving
    exactly here,
    exactly now,
    exactly you.
Every superhero has an origin story,
    And this one is yours.

Because after all, 14 billion years is an awfully long time
to grow someone, so there must be a good reason.

It's up to you to find out what that is.

075 Julia

Julia was 99 years old when she passed. She said she wasn't afraid. She said she had faith, and I believed her.

Three months before she passed at the age of 99, she wheeled herself out from her back room and over to her piano where I was practicing. She said she didn't hear something that she should. She said she suspected that one of my fingers wasn't doing its job.

A year before she passed at the age of 99, we were looking at a piece of music by Ravel when she shouted, "Oh my word! I've been thinking about this the wrong way for fifty years!" She laughed and laughed, and then abandoned fifty years of certainty and changed how she thought without even a hint of hesitation.

About four years before she passed at the age of 99, Julia was disgusted with the state of elder care in Pennsylvania, and having previously struggled with the treatment of her late husband, she decided that she'd do something about it. With the help of some committed friends, local attorneys, and Penn State Law students, she succeeded in having legislation drafted in the state of Pennsylvania to protect seniors from unfair or faulty contracts.

About fifty years before she passed at the age of 99, Julia turned pages for Artur Rubinstein while he recorded Beethoven and Brahms concerti with the Boston Symphony Orchestra. He caught her looking at his hands during a particularly difficult passage, and said to her, "You want to know how I do those thirds?" She nodded her head, and he whispered from the side of his mouth, "I cheat." He sent her roses once the sessions were finished with a note that read, "I place these at your feet."

About sixty years before she passed at the age of 99, Julia was driving to the airport to begin a tour of South America for RCA Victor, who had signed her to their roster of performing artists. Her car was rear-ended at a tollbooth and the impact broke her back, ending her career as a concert pianist. After a long rehabilitation, Julia decided to teach, which is how I met her decades later.

Sometime long before Julia passed at the age of 99, before any of these events and before any of the others—like flying planes, recording a weekly radio show, having a large family, and receiving countless teaching awards and honors—Julia decided that life was to be lived.

Julia continues to teach to this day.

076 Five Little Things to Remember

Someday, if everything goes exactly as it should—

I will grow old . . .
    and everyone I love will grow old,
    and everyone I don't love will grow old,
    and everyone I don't know and will never meet will grow old,
    and there is no escape from this
        (if everything goes just as it should).

I will get sick . . .
    and everyone I love will get sick,
    and everyone I don't love will get sick,
    and everyone I don't know and will never meet will get sick,
    and there is no escape from this
        (if everything goes just as it should).

I will die . . .
    and everyone I love will die,
    and everyone I don't love will die,
    and everyone I don't know and will never meet will die,
    and there is no escape from this
        (if everything goes just as it should).

I will have to let go of everything that is dear to me . . .
    and of everything I own
    and of everything I have ever owned,
    and of everything that I have wanted but never acquired,
    and there is no escape from this
        (if everything goes just as it should).

I alone own my actions . . .
    I am their heir.
    I am their descendant.
    I am what I put out, for good or for evil,
    I am the consequences.

What I do matters.
What I do shapes the world.
What I put forth, I am.

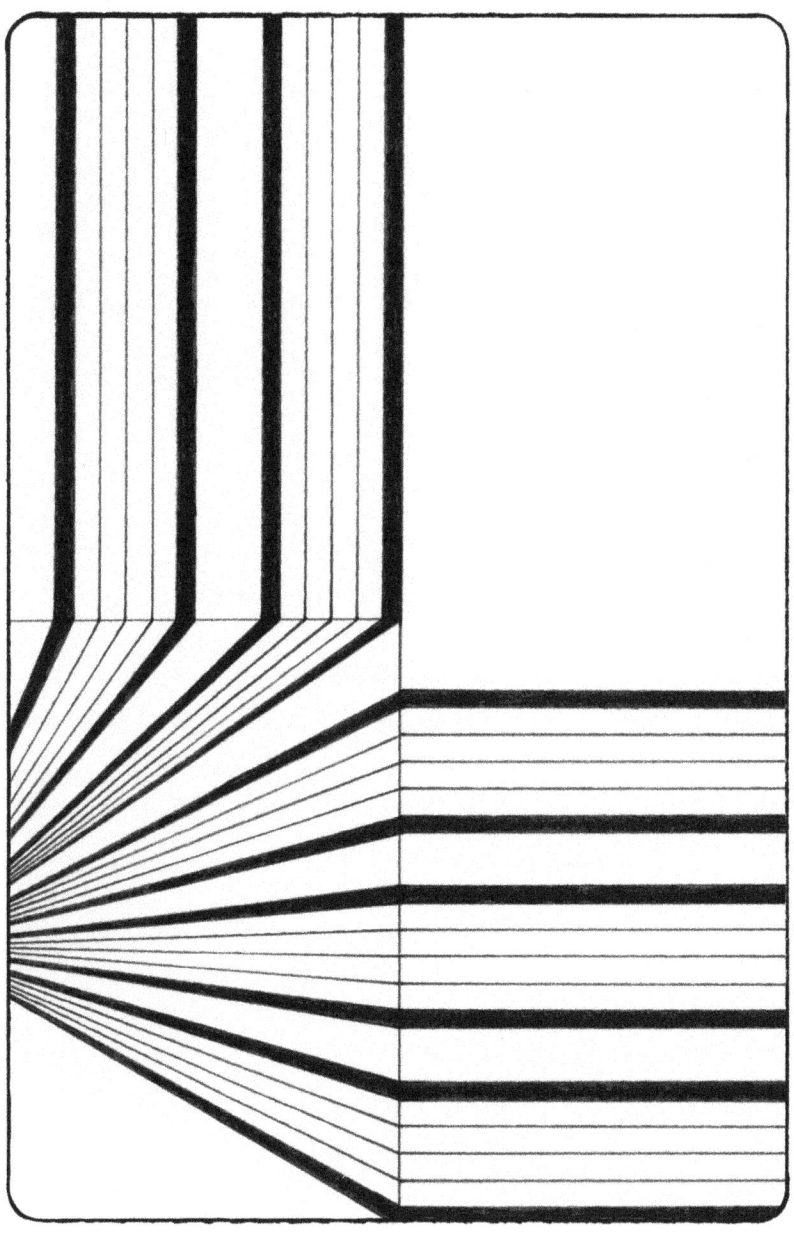

How, Not What

A friend of mine told me that they knew some stuff about manifestation. They said that they'd witnessed people making things come true by putting their intentions "out into the universe," and they said that there is some extra magic to it if you write it down. They said it's like some sort of contract with the universe: Write the intention down, and the universe will take care of the rest.

I didn't know if I believed it, but I also didn't not believe it. I make it a policy of mine to never believe anything at a full 100%, which means that I also never disbelieve anything at a full 100%. The universe is just too filled with mystery to be absolutely confident about anything, and besides, the moment I grip something at 100%, then I no longer have any room to move, to bob and weave. Even 99% belief gives me 1% to learn, change, and adapt, so that's what I go with.

Anyway, I figured I'd give it a shot. What could it hurt? Besides, I had an upcoming professional thing that I really wanted to go well, so I wrote down exactly what I wanted:

- I want people to come to my thing.
- I want people to benefit from what I have to offer.
- I want to benefit from their benefitting from it, but in a cool and totally non-jerky way. Not selfish-like, but you know, I want good stuff to come from it to me.
- I want it to be successful.

Over the next few days, I started to keep an eye out for signs that it was working. I didn't see anything at first, but then someone signed up (and paid)! Holy shit! Someone signed up! And paid! Then someone else signed-up, too! OH MY FREAKING GOSH! IT'S WORKING!

Then some days went by and . . .

and nobody else signed up.

And then some more days went by . . .

And then I started to feel anxious. A little, at first, and then more so. I started to do stuff to encourage people to come (ads, social media posts, etc.), but it didn't seem to help, and I started to get nervous that it was all going to be a big failure and soon I couldn't think about much else except how embarrassed and stupid I was going to feel to be at an event with only two people (if they even showed up at all). I could see the person hosting the event looking at me with disappointment, or even worse, pity. I started to think about how this manifestation thing was clearly some sort of new age bullshit sham, and even if it wasn't, it wasn't worth the price of the anxiety of waiting for the universe to get off its ass and do its part. I mean, was the universe just too busy? Did it have too many other contracts to fulfill? I mean, with all the suffering in the world, what right did I have to ask for anything?

So I gave up on it. I found the paper on which I wrote my wishes and I scratched them out.

But like I mentioned before, I didn't throw out the idea of manifestation completely, I only threw it out about 98% (maybe 96%). Under my scratch-outs, I was inspired to write something new.

I wrote:
- I want to stop thinking that I need anything at all—that I need to manifest anything whatsoever.
- I want to let go of thinking I need to be improved in any way.
- I want my life to be about how I am instead of what I do or have.

And the universe seemed to answer right away. The very next day I noticed some things: I noticed a leaf fall from a tree and spin like a top all the way to the ground, like a little drill burrowing through the air. I noticed a barred owl hooting from what seemed like a million miles away, only to be answered by another a million and one miles further. I noticed my wife helping my mom get to her chemo appointment, and I also noticed her kissing our little dog on her furry head as she was stealing a nap on top of our bed, and in all of them, my heart felt like it was pirouetting in my chest with wonder and awe and thankfulness, and a question boomed in my head:

> Is it like this all the time?
> Does this stuff happen every day?

And I knew without question that it did. I knew that it did to the point of breaking my policy: I knew it 100%, just as I also knew that it had worked, that I (along with the universe, of course) had manifested this.

Suddenly how the event went no longer mattered so much, because I knew to my core that the event was already a success, no matter who came or what happened. I had the universe in my heart, pirouetting away, and a word like failure seemed like something I no longer found all that necessary.

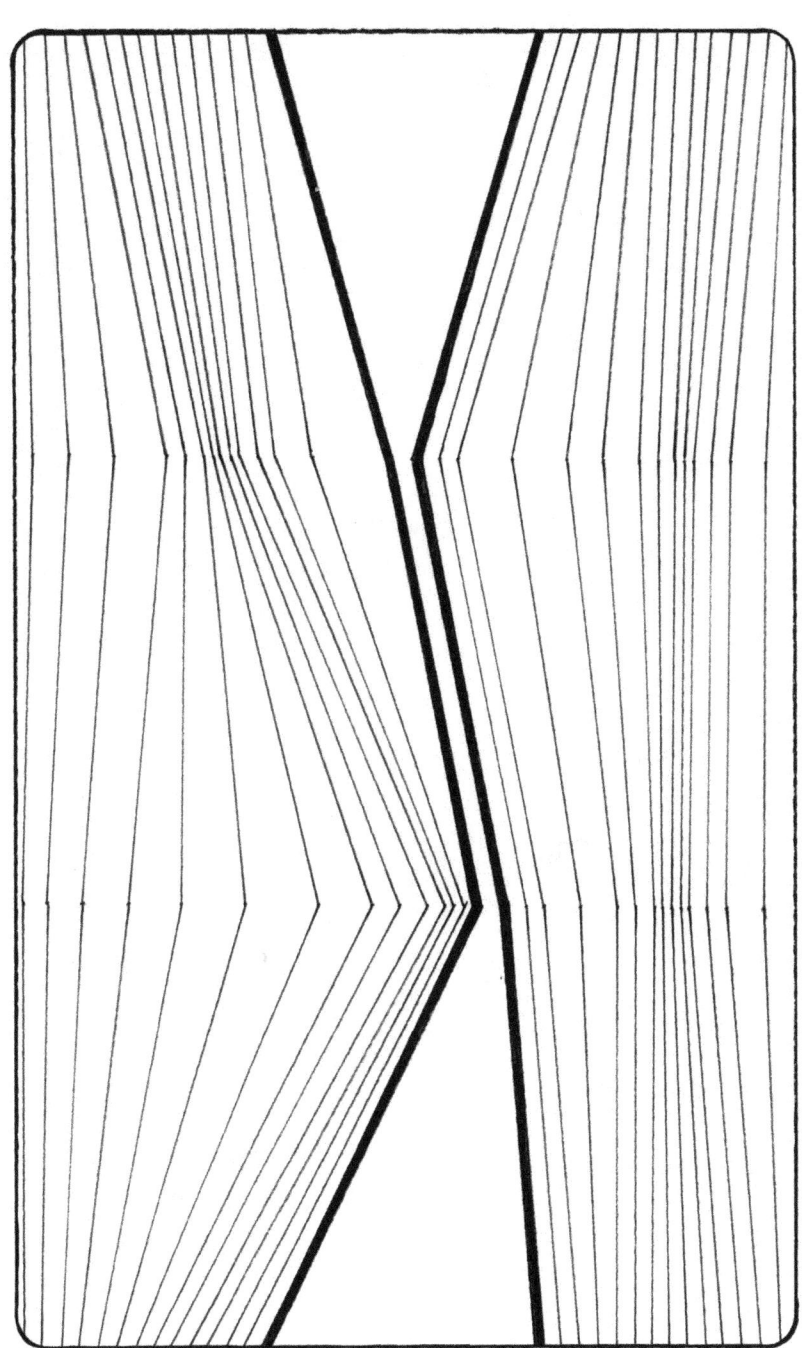

078

A Heavy Load

Once upon a time, two monks were walking along a trail through the forest when they came to a muddy stream running across their path.

Standing at the stream's bank was a young woman who was unable to move. She was wearing a very beautiful kimono and there was no way she was going to make it across without ruining the bottom of it. Without saying a word, the older of the two monks grabbed the woman and picked her up, splashed his way across the stream, and put her down on the other side.

As she hurried along her way, the younger monk was horrified: one doesn't just grab young women, especially if one is a monk! The young monk could not escape the thought that what the older monk did was absolutely unthinkable.

For some time afterward, the two walked quietly side by side, but the younger monk continued to stew and simmer and boil until finally he couldn't take it anymore, shouting:

> **How could you do that?!**
> **You just grabbed that woman!**
> **You! A monk!**
> **Do you have any idea how inappropriate that was!**
> **What if someone saw you?**
> **What if someone saw me with you!**
> **What were you thinking!?**

The older monk thought for a moment and said, "Your arms must be very, very tired."

The young monk shot back, "What? Why would my arms be tired?" to which the older monk replied, "Well, I put that woman down hours ago, but you? You're still carrying her."

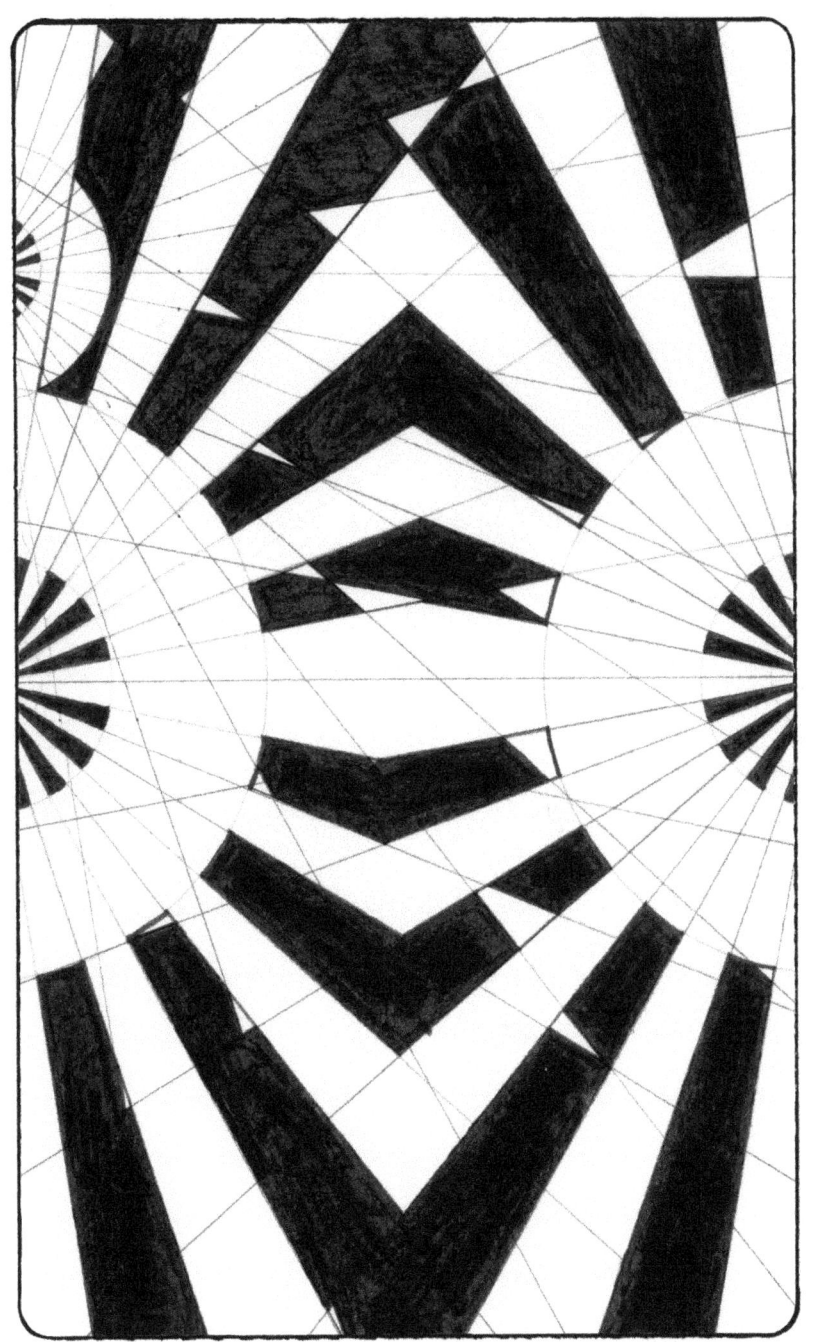

It was a beautiful day and I wanted to get the lawn done
quickly, but as I took the mower out, I had a crazy feeling
that I was going to accidentally run over a little animal.
Growing up in the country around farms and hunters,
I'm no stranger to death as a very regular part of life, but
I just can't stand the thought of it happening because
of my own carelessness or unconsciousness.

So, I asked the Bodhisattva Jizo for help. Jizo cares
for children and animals, as well as travelers and expectant
mothers. He's usually depicted as a cheerful little guy with
a bald head and a monk's robe. He carries a staff and has
a jewel in his forehead that he uses to light the way for all
those who need him. I asked Jizo to please protect all of the
little animals, and I invoked him by quietly repeating
his mantra:

Namo Jizo Bosa, Namo Jizo Bosa, Namo Jizo Bosa.

About fifteen minutes into mowing, the tiniest bunny I ever
saw squirmed out from under a bush and ran right in front
of the machine. It was so small that it could hardly hop—
it was kind of half hopping, half crawling. Thankfully, I saw it
and was able to stop just inches away. Not ten minutes later,
I caught a flash from the corner of my eye and a beautiful
adult garter snake burst from some pachysandra and almost
ended up right under the mower. Instinctively, I disengaged
the mower blades and swerved, allowing my reptilian pal
to quickly make its way into the nearby forest.

Reflecting on it afterwards, I wondered three questions
to myself:

Did Jizo intervene? I indeed asked for his help, and in review,
I might say that he seemed to tip me off right in the nick
of time for both of them.

Or . . .

Did my actions alone save them? In other words, my prayer and chant to Jizo didn't conjure anything supernatural or paranormal, they were just mindful tools that helped me to be extra conscious of my environment and my place in it, and to be ready to act when I needed to.

But the third question is the real puzzle—the one that really bakes my noodle: Is there any difference between questions one and two?

080 Letting Go

I hold my suffering in tight white knuckles. My fists
clench my regret, embarrassment, guilt, hurtful
memories, and fear so tightly that it's like they become
me—like they *are* me.

I want to let them drop away. I want to turn my fist
over, open my fingers, and let them fall to the ground.
I want to be done with them forever, but I can't remove
a memory or a fear from my mind any more than I could
remove my brain or heart. I can't "just drop it."

Instead, I keep my fist turned upward, and I open
my fingers. I let go, not by dropping, but by seeing.
I look at the suffering resting in my palm.

In unclenching, I release it as a part of me. In seeing it,
I acknowledge what seemed to once be true. I watch it and
understand how it may have shaped me. I keep vigil with
it as I intentionally choose a path of my own making, one
supported by the wisdom of what I've learned.

I no longer wish it to fall away from me. It's part
of my path, and while painful (maybe incredibly so),
my suffering and I came to this moment together.

I remember that the beauty of the lotus flower isn't
despite the mud from which it grows, but rather because
of it. I honor my story as a tapestry of my life, and I bow
to every moment of it.

I open my palm, I see my suffering—and then I choose.

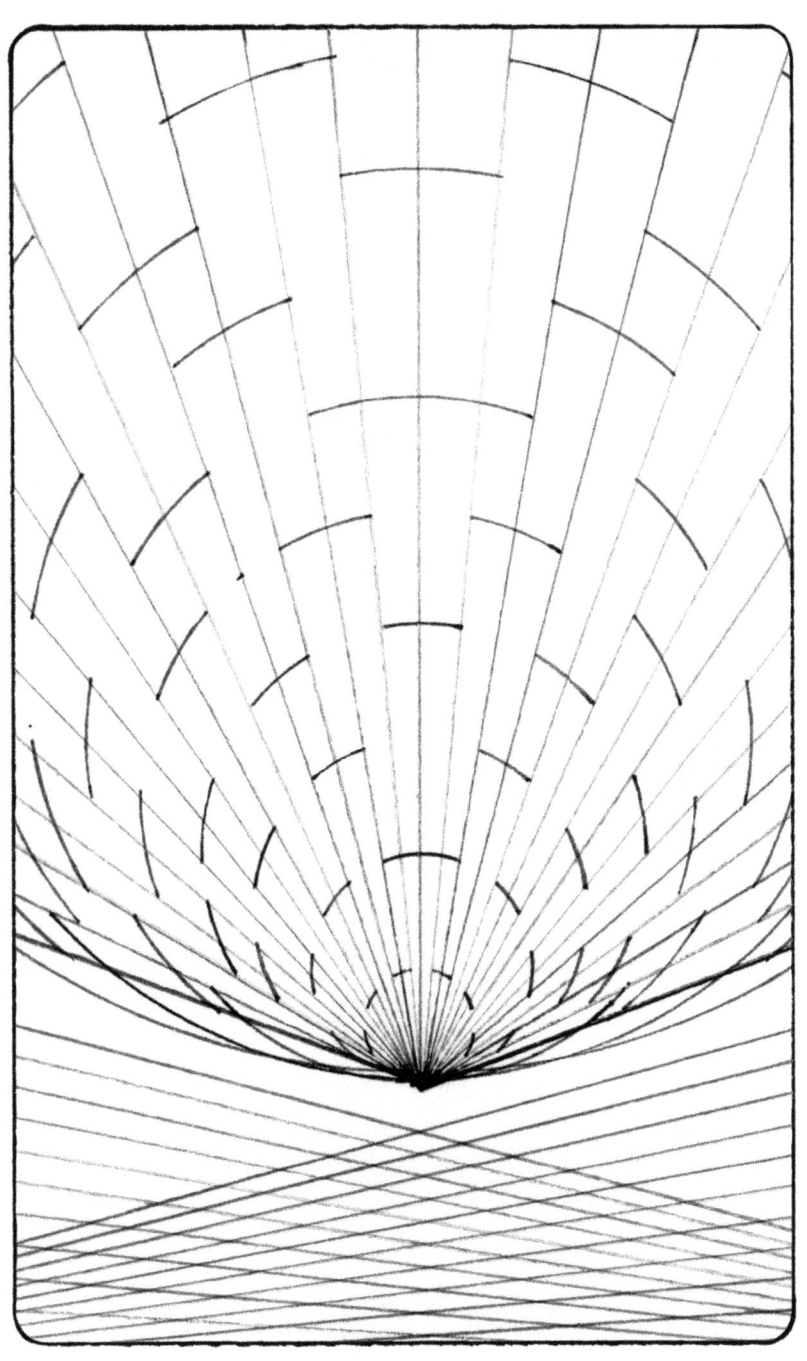

081 Synchronicity

I was about three miles into the hike when I happened upon the raccoons. They immediately high-tailed it around a tree and disappeared, but I knew they were still watching me. Not ten minutes later, I had a similar run-in with a beautiful doe having a drink. With a handful of graceful leaps, she put sixty feet between us and then stopped, stone-still, save for the flicker of her white tail.

Sometime later, I encountered something entirely new: a sound that I could not identify. It sounded like someone very loudly and rhythmically raking leaves in bursts of three: PHH! PHH! PHH! Or were they breaths? My sympathetic nervous system decided for me, and I froze in place and listened. Again: PHH! PHH! PHH! With this second round, I had no doubt that whatever it was, it was deliberate. Recalling the empty parking area and my current depth within the state game lands, I was fairly confident it wasn't human. Maybe it was a buck? Maybe a turkey? Maybe a black bear? I've since listened to quite a few YouTube clips of various fauna snorting, foraging, rutting, etc., and nothing seems to match. I clapped my hands and smacked a stick against a tree, figuring there's no sense in trying to hide, electing for "I'm here and I make loud noises, too!" After a few minutes of basking in my very naked and exposed humanity, I made my way along the trail.

About 40 minutes later, I spotted a buck. He was big and beautiful, and he thundered away in five or six loud strides that I could feel in my feet. Like the raccoons and the doe, I heard him stop and could sense him watching me, waiting to see what I was or what I would do. It almost felt like he was mocking me, saying, "Make no mistake, we know you're here. All of us."

I mention this incident as a reminder. Whatever I may be doing—pouring milk on cereal, getting gas, running reports, sitting on a train—a very different life is out there, and it's not always something I understand. It's under waves, it's in grasslands, it's in trees and above them: a whole other world where I am far from in control, and it's all happening right now. As I type this and as you read it, it's there, reminding me that the veil between the life that I think I control and something much wilder is very thin.

There is magic in remembering this (in the very least, there's humility). It forces me to recognize how often I spend my time looking at life as through the cardboard center of a toilet paper roll, when all the while there is vastly more that is interacting, influencing, and shaping the world of which I am only one single expression.

The Genjokoan of the Turtles

I knew not to get too close. Snapping turtles are famous for their bad tempers and—of course, the snap that is their namesake—but I also had a dilemma. The huge one in my backyard seemed to be headed towards the creek, which is about 40 yards away, but to get there, they'd have to make their way down a very steep hill, and worse, across a very busy back road, so I felt pulled to somehow help it on its journey. I knew that handling a large snapping turtle can be dangerous if you don't know what you're doing (and I didn't), and I couldn't be positive that the creek was its destination, anyway. In the end, I chose to let the turtle be in control of its own turtle destiny, thinking that it would know how to survive in its world better than I would.

A couple of hours later, I found myself second-guessing my decision. I should have helped that turtle. I know that road well, and it is only reasonable to conclude that it was headed for the creek. I was therefore floored with guilt when, as I was driving home from the store, I came across a recently struck large turtle at the bottom of the hill from my house. I felt absolutely terrible— "I did this. I killed that turtle." I replayed my thinking a million times and reminded myself that it had been a conscious decision. I had considered helping, but using the best logic I had at the time, purposefully decided against it, even though I knew the potential consequences. But none of my retrospective logic did any good. I felt tremendously guilty.

Two days later I was walking on a path through the woods behind our home, still reflecting on what had happened. With advice from my family and some focused mindfulness practice, I was able to lessen some of the guilt, reminding myself that I can only take responsibility for what I can control, and that the amount of control I have over a snapping turtle is limited to say the least. I was able to start letting go of the story that I directly caused that turtle's demise, but it still lingered.

I decided that if I were ever in that situation again, that I would grab my heaviest work gloves, and I would somehow get it to the creek. I'd talk to my good pal, Scott, who is a herpetology professor, and I'd learn how to pick one up. Next time, I'd be prepared.

As I walked along the path, about a half of a mile away from my home, I came across another snapping turtle. Not quite as large as the one in my yard, but still something to see. I bowed to it and wished it well. Much to my surprise, I then came across another one not but 50 feet away from the first: both of them headed in the direction of my house and toward the creek! When I came across a third even closer to my house, I started to quicken my pace. I began to nervously wonder, "Is this some kind of 'great turtle migration'?" Paranoia started to creep in, and I began to have visions of getting to my house, only to discover thirty, forty, maybe hundreds upon hundreds of large snapping turtles, all in my backyard, all at the top of the steep hill, all needing to make it across that deadly road, all waiting for me.

083　The Wisdom in Our Challenges

Once upon a time, at the foot of a beautiful mountain, in front of a beautiful stream, in a beautiful forest, there was a monastery where monks peacefully practiced meditation, lived joyfully in the ever-present now, and felt deeply at One with all things. Guiding the monks was the wisest master in the land, and they all lived together in perfect, blissful harmony.

One day a new monk arrived. He was "different" from the others. He was loud, rude, and obnoxious. He let his hair grow far too long, and he never bathed. When the monks quietly ate their meals, he slurped his bowl loudly, belched boorishly, and never cleaned up afterward. During meditation, he would snort noisily, scratch disruptively, and break wind noxiously.

The other monks couldn't help themselves. Despite their sacred vows and precepts, they hated him! He ruined their blissful paradise of tranquility and peace, and after several weeks, they couldn't take it anymore, and they decided that something had to be done. They decided that they had to get rid of him!

After discussing a plan, they gathered what little money they had from the sale of vegetables from the monastery garden and gave all of it to a local villager to kidnap the obnoxious monk and take him far away—so far that he'd never find his way back to their beautiful home.

Well, it worked! Almost immediately, the monastery returned to the perfect image of serenity that it had once been. With a melodic sigh of relief, the monks faced no more annoyances, no more challenges, no more farts. All was wonderful.

After several days, the master noticed that that new monk was missing, and asked, "Where is he?" The other monks, knowing in their hearts that kidnapping wasn't exactly a monk-like thing to do, fessed-up and told the master what they had done.

Trying to remain calm, the master asked, "You paid to have him taken away?" They guiltily bowed their heads and meekly replied, "Yes," to which the master responded,

"Well you better go find him! I'm paying him to be here!"

The master truly was wise.
He knew that there is no great feat or skill in peacefulness of mind when there is no threat to having one.

084 Everyone Buddha

Everyone has Buddha Nature,
>the seed of enlightenment, the capacity to awaken
>to the True Nature of all things:
>To end all delusions.
>To fully embody wisdom and compassion.
>To end suffering for themselves and for all beings.

Every one of us is on the path:
>We may simply need time or opportunity
>or the compassion of others to know it.

If I look really carefully, though, I can see it.
>Look!

There's Buddha!
>The teeny tiny baby desperately trying to fit their
>whole foot in their mouth.

There's Buddha!
>The nurse coming off a double-shift to an empty house.

There's Buddha!
>The addict looking to unload the copper they stole
>from under the sign that read, "Don't Steal My Scrap!"

There's Buddha!
>The executive responsible for earnings that exceeded
>projections and for dismissing 6,000 employees two
>weeks before Christmas.

There's Buddha!
>The beloved kid's baseball coach stumbling from a bar
>and getting behind the wheel of a car.

There's Buddha!
>The father who killed that beautiful, endangered rhino
>for its horn so that he could feed his starving family.

There's Buddha!
> The mother in the garden, missing her children
> now grown and moved away, but grateful for their
> happiness and safety.

Every one of us, Buddha.
> May we all come to know it.

A Glimpse of Enlightenment

The following is a glimpse of enlightenment:

Two muffins were baking in an oven. One muffin says to the other, "Boy, it's hot in here," to which the other muffin replies, "Oh my gosh! A talking muffin!"

How!? How can a silly joke be a "glimpse of enlightenment?" Well . . .

First, over billions of years, what was mostly hydrogen cooled and started to form nebulae and stars which become the forges for materials that would eventually become our planet. At some point, simple protein structures formed from non-organic materials, which then came to life as more complex multicellular organisms. These organisms continued to grow and change and diversity, eventually developing the astounding abilities of complex communication, self-awareness, and curiosity about how everything came to be, and deep questions about why. As part of this journey, they developed the ability to feel emotions, such as joy, sorrow, wonder, and humor. This silly joke is a culmination of all that came to be, and deep questions about why. As part of this journey, they developed the ability to feel emotions, such as joy, sorrow, wonder, and humor. This silly joke is a culmination of all that came before it, and deep questions about influenced it, and all that created everything that is, which I comprehend by being part of it. What's more, I get it in the blink of an eye—I embody all of this without any effort whatsoever. If I'm not paying attention, then this joke is dull and mundane and I move on with my day. If I am paying attention, though, then I laugh, and then I bow.

House on Fire

Once upon a time when I was fairly sure I was enlightened, I was leading an online meditation that was disrupted by a most vile and unwelcome guest—an internet troll. In the middle of a particularly wise and well-delivered breathy stream of peaceful calmness, a voice boomed from the ether with a barrage of obscenities that are now lost to me, save for one particular word that my friends on the call will lovingly never let me forget: "hammercock."

Thankfully, I understood what was happening, so I had the wherewithal to quickly eject the intruder, re-establish a safe environment for the participants, and complete the session. We were even able to leverage the event in our practice, because wouldn't you know it, the topic of the day was, "Dealing with Difficulty." Looking back, I'm thankful that it wasn't worse than it was, as they could have projected or said something truly offensive, racist, or harmful. I think we got off lucky.

But hours later, despite all my most I'm-pretty-sure-I'm-enlightened efforts, I could still feel it—deeply. My adrenaline was still coursing, my blood pressure was still high, and my anger was still running at 9,000 RPMs. I thought I had done everything possible to make peace with it: I meditated, I exercised, I went for a long walk, and I scoured the internet to see if I could find that no-good son-of-a-gun, so I could . . . I'm not sure what.

What I discovered, though, is that the louder I told these thoughts, feelings, and sensations to go away, the louder they got. The more I reminded myself that I was a fully ordained Buddhist priest who should be able to simply raise a flower to these thoughts and have them smile back at me, the more they paced and stomped and screamed.

Finally, I broke. Out of desperation more than anything else, I turned towards the thoughts and yelled back: "What?! What do you want?!" And boy-oh-boy did they answer: "We're not good! We're not OK! That troll could have really hurt someone, and we didn't do nearly enough to protect them! Enlightened Buddhist priest? Ha! We're a fraud! We're shit! We're an embarrassment! We're a failure! We should have never quit our corporate job! We should run away! We should disappear!"

Listening, I was struck by how frantic the voice was—how panicked—and my heart broke for it. It was truly suffering. It was truly scared.

An image popped into my head, one of myself watching TV, and someone I love bursting into the room, yelling, "I think the house is on fire! We have to get out!" I imagined how that voice might sound if I were to reply, "Could you please get out of here? I'm trying to watch this."

"ARE YOU OUT OF YOUR MIND?! LISTEN TO ME! THE HOUSE IS ON FIRE! WE NEED TO GET OUT!"

I realized that this was exactly what I was doing to that voice within me now, and I reflexively turned toward it, grabbed it with a huge hug, and said, "Oh my gosh, pal, you're OK! I got you! You're safe!"

I realized that, instead of pushing that voice away, I needed to let it say what it needed to say. I needed to let it feel what it needed to feel. I needed to sit with it like I was its very best friend—I needed to care for it. The content of what it offered wasn't helpful, true, or something I was going to act on, but it was only when it knew it was safe that it could begin to extinguish its fire and listen to a wiser story of what happened.

Nowadays, I'm fairly sure of very little. I'm getting better, however, at keeping an eye out for whoever may visit my mind, and when they're frightened, remembering that maybe I don't have to hate or push them away. Maybe I can care for them. Maybe when the house is on fire, I can make sure that they know they don't have to bear the burden of keeping us safe by themselves. Maybe I can make sure they know that they're OK, that I've got them, and that they're safe.

087

Finding an Inner Voice That's True

Call to mind someone who, the moment you think of them,
fills your whole chest and belly and soul with warmth
and love.

Picture them clearly in your mind and heart.
　　A best friend,
　　A child,
　　A grandparent,
　　An aunt or uncle,
　　A dog or a cat.

Give yourself permission for this being to be a sure thing:
　　If you think it should be someone in your family but
　　wish it could be the dog that you had when you were
　　a child but who has been gone for years, go with your
　　dog. Pay no mind to whether this being is still with
　　us or not. After all, just because someone is no longer
　　here doesn't mean that they've forgotten about you.

With them in your heart and mind, imagine that whatever
challenge you're facing or struggling with is actually
happening to them, and then ask yourself,
　　How would I show up for them?
　　What would I say to them?
　　How would I comfort them?
　　How would I advise them?

Now turn this same voice
and all of its advice, care, lessons, comfort, and love
towards yourself,
and as best as you can,
listen to it.

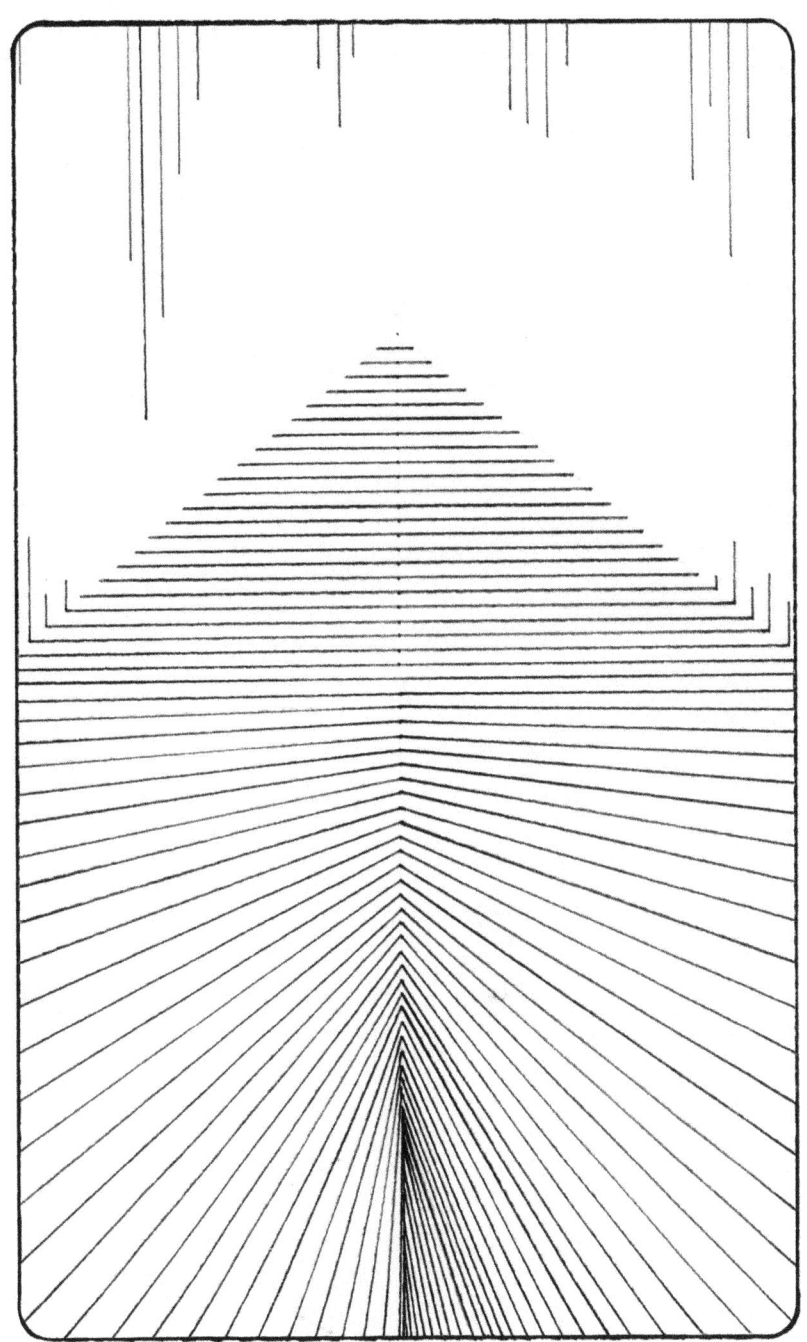

088

Taking In & Sending Out

I shut my eyes and I ask myself—
What do I need most?
What would make a difference if I had it within
me at this moment?

Am I stressed and need comfort?
Am I fearful and need courage?
Am I despairing and need light in the darkness?

Despite the heaviness I may feel, I remember that
I have the heart of a Buddha, and I ask it to open.
I ask the Buddha within me to awaken.

With my eyes shut, I picture my hurting self sitting
across from me. I picture them as though they are truly
there. I picture them with a certainty that if I opened
my eyes, I'd most certainly see myself there.

With my heart awakened and full, I breathe in the hurt
sitting across from me. I picture it swirling from
my hurting self like a black, thick smoke.

I take it into my awakened heart, and on my out-breath,
I return it transformed: a golden healing light. No longer
a black smoke, I return the light of exactly what my hurting
self yearns for: comfort, courage, lightness, ease, and love.

With each breath, I transform and am transformed.

I then turn to all beings everywhere, and knowing that
they suffer as I do, I offer the same golden light.

I take in the hurt of every child soldier in Africa,
Every grandmother in Naples, Italy (and Naples, Florida),
Every teenager in Brazil,
Every divorced, single parent in Australia,
Everyone, everywhere.

And I send it out as golden light.
I take in the hurt of the world,
And I send it out as golden light.

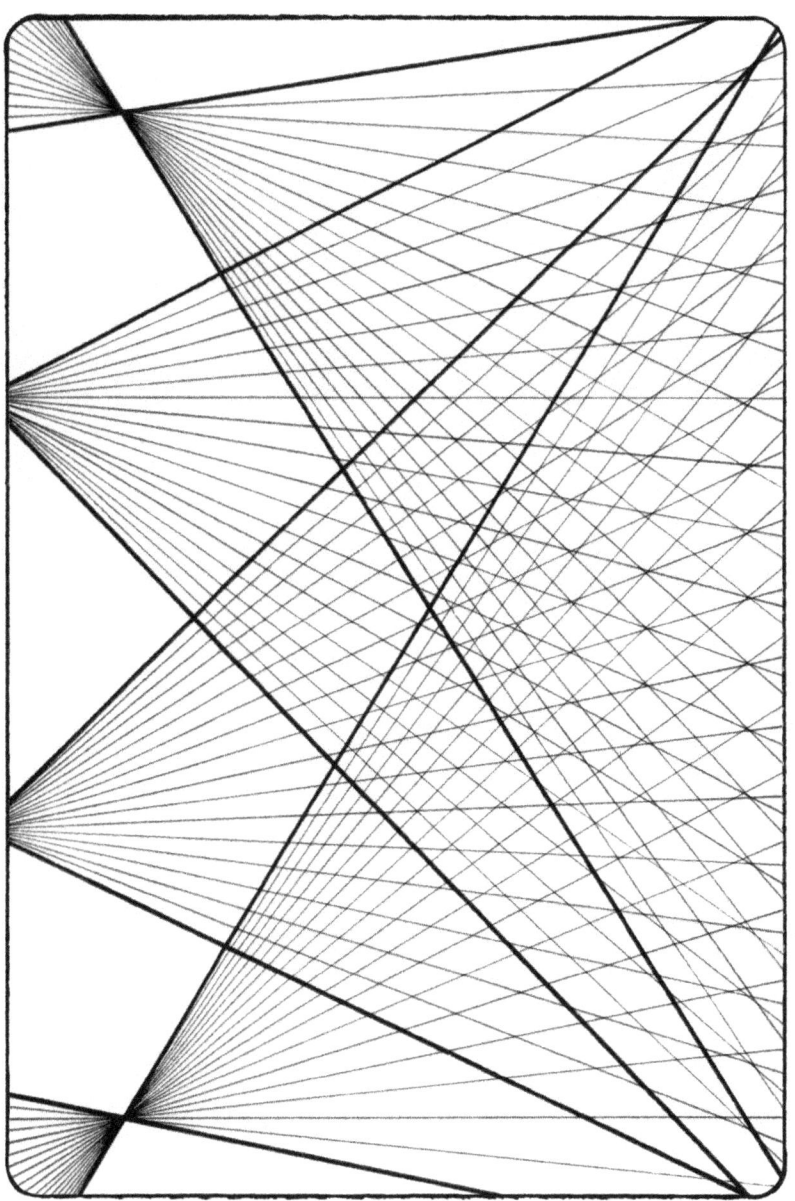

089　Prayer Wheel

I have a small prayer wheel that I spin like a top each morning. Inside the wheel is a scroll with the same Sanskrit phrase repeated over and over:

　　Om Mani Padme Hum

In spinning the wheel, waves upon waves of this sacred prayer spiral outward to all beings everywhere, across all space and time—each revolution a chorus of thousands reciting it from countless mountaintops.

Om is the holy sound of the universe, itself.
Mani (jewel) Padme (lotus) is the Jeweled-Lotus of compassion, herself, the Bodhisattva Avalokitesvara/ GuanYin/Kanzeon.
Hum is the sound of my heart opening for all beings everywhere and everywhen.

Each syllable aligns with the six Perfections, the Paramitas:

　　Om is generosity,
　　Ma is virtue,
　　Ni is patience,
　　Pad is energy,
　　Me is concentration,
　　Hum is the sound of my heart opening for all beings. . .

Each sound is inherently empty without the existence of the others. Each syllable is a reminder of my True Self, my Buddha Nature, my connection to all there is, was, and will be—a reminder that I am that.

(Here. Now you have one, too. . .)

INSTRUCTIONS:

1. Lay on a
flat surface.
2. Spin.

090 Fudo

Fudo's wallet is the one that says "bad motherfucker" on it.

The Bodhisattva Fudo Myo-o is pitch black and has eyes
that are so blood-red that they glow. His fangs snaggle out
of his mouth on opposite sides, and he carries a rope that
he uses to bind all delusions, and a sword to cut them.
Fudo chains his ankle to wherever he's called to show his
commitment to remain until all delusions are extinguished
and all beings are safe.

Fudo is known as "The Immovable One."

Fudo is a Bodhisattva of Protection and Safety,
a Dharmapala—protector of the Dharma.

Summoning Fudo is practical: If you need to fight the biggest
and baddest monsters there are, then you call the biggest
and baddest monster there is to back you up.

Fudo's mantra offers prayers of safety and protection.

> Namo Fudo Bosa
> Namo Fudo Bosa
> Namo Fudo Bosa

I chant Fudo's mantra as I invite the scariest of my Hungry
Ghosts to show themselves, so that I may have the courage
to face them and feed them—so that I may love them.

I chant Fudo's mantra when my kiddo takes the car and
before my wife's visit to the doctor.

I chant his mantra when I'm fearful or anxious.

I chant his mantra for all beings who are scared, facing
the unknown, or finding themselves in dark places.

Like all Bodhisattvas, Fudo is a metaphor. Fudo is the courage, steadfastness, and power that exists within all of us already.

Fudo is a reminder that there isn't anything between my fear and myself, that there is only ever one thing.

I am Fudo.

091 The Thought Is Not the Thing

The thought of the moon is not the moon.
  To know the moon, I have to look into the sky and see it.

The thought of a strawberry is not a strawberry.
  To know a strawberry, I have to taste it.

The thought of a job is not the job.
  To know a job, I have to work.

The thought of a friendship is not a friendship.
  To know a friendship, I have to be a friend.

The thought of exhaustion is not exhaustion.
  To know exhaustion, I have to feel exhaustion.

The thought of music is not music.
  To know music, I have to listen.

The thought of a dance is not dancing.
  To know a dance, I have to dance.

The thought of laughter is not laughter.
  To know laughter, I have to laugh.

The thought of who I am is not who I am.
  To know who I am, I have to be.

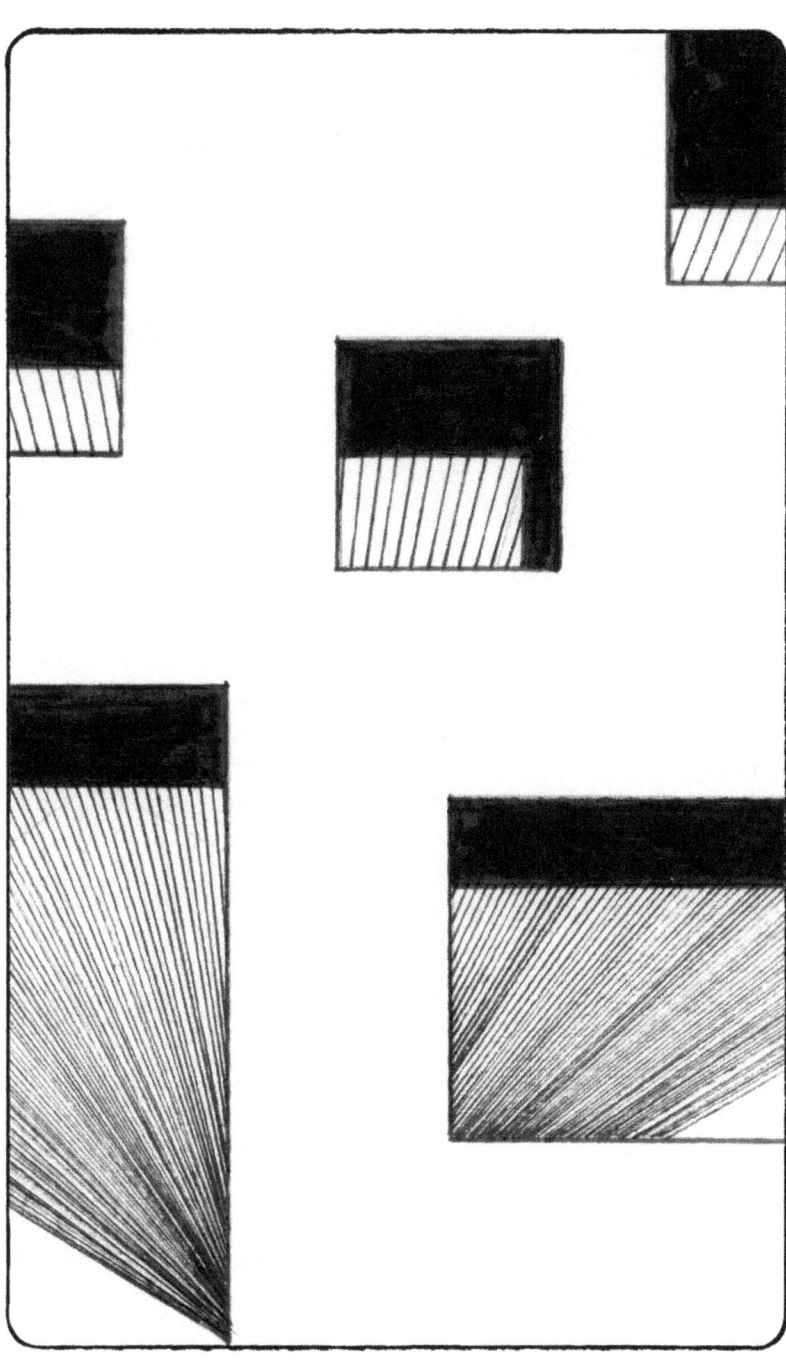

Words! Words!
The Way is beyond language, Words never could, cannot now, and never
will describe the Way.
—Seng-ts'an, Third Patriarch of Zen, from the **Verses on the**
Perfect Mind (Hsin-Hsin Ming)

I'm very grateful for words. Words help me to share
experiences and understanding with others, but even
the most precise definitions are only an approximation
of what's really true. Nothing is ever only what it seems.
That giant thing I call a tree is also the sun, the water, the
air, and the ground upon which it depends, as well as the
squirrel who delivered it to where it rests when it was
so small that it could fit in the palm of any hand.

It's important that I remember words' limitations.
It's important that I remember that while they mean one
thing to me, they may mean something very different
to others. For example:

> What is 'freedom'?
> What is 'right'?
> What is 'love'?

To answer these questions with certainty would be to build
walls around what's infinitely high—to contain
the uncontainable.

It's important that I remember to hold words like a sleeping
baby or a tiny bird.

Words are depended upon to keep us all safe and connected,
just as they are used to drive each other apart.

Words are used to point to the indescribable so it may touch us all and end our suffering,
    just as they are used to cause suffering.

Words are used to define how to live together peacefully,
    just as they are used to justify how some must die.

Bowing to words' power, I vow to use words skillfully and to hold them reverently.

I vow to be as precise as possible, and to allow for the spaciousness that words inherently require.

093 Bob and Weave

A clay Buddha cannot cross water.
A bronze Buddha cannot get through a furnace.
A wooden Buddha cannot get through a fire.
—Zen Master Joshu

Hold plans loosely.
Abandon expectations. Abandon certainty.
Remember people more than plans.
Remember hearts more than doing.
Plan, plot, strategize, calculate, and
Hold loosely.

Hold conversations loosely.
Abandon winning. Abandon losing.
Don't rehearse on a stage. Don't fight in an arena.
Listen, respond, advocate, inquire, and
Hold loosely.

Hold life loosely.
Abandon the thought that you need anything.
Abandon the thought that you need nothing.
Give a wide berth for what comes.
Give a wide berth for what goes.
Work hard, (for)give, laugh, grieve, and
Hold loosely.

Cross the water, and then leave the boat on the shore.
There's no need to carry it on your back afterward.

Bob and weave,
Bob and weave,
Bob and weave.

094 Breathe and Become

I picture exactly who I need—

> exactly who I wish that I was,
> exactly who would know exactly what to do when I don't.

> Maybe they are the picture of wisdom, compassion, and
> calmness: They are Kanzeon. They are Martin Luther
> King, Jr. They are Thich Nhat Hanh.

> Maybe they are the picture of courage, steadfastness,
> and confidence: They are Fudo. They are Wonder Woman.
> They are Jesse Owens.

> Maybe they are the picture of peace, light, and
> selflessness: They are Jesus Christ. They are Buddha.

I close my eyes and I picture them. I picture them sitting
across from me as real as anything has ever been real. I keep
my eyes shut, but I know with certainty that if I opened
them, they would be sitting there—right in front of me.

They're here. They're with me. They're here to help me.
They're clear. They're supporting me. They're pulling for me.
Their light is my light.

With each in-breath,
I breathe in their presence,
allowing it to fill every part of my entire being like pouring
water into a vase.
I breathe in until there isn't a space within me that isn't them.
I breathe in until we are One.

And then, together as One, we open our eyes.
And together as One, we step forward.

095   Instructions to the Chief Cook

In a 1,000-year-old set of instructions to the chief cook of a
Zen monastery, they are advised to "Take up the leaf of a green
vegetable, and turn it into a towering golden body."

In Zen, everything is sacred exactly as it is:
the most foul and the most beautiful,
all manifestations of the singular profound nature of being.

Every
statue, mountain stream, old piece of trash, sprig of pine,
or act of chopping a head of romaine
is an expression of our single shared Ground of Being.

Everything, everywhere:
the arranging of flowers, the performing of a dance,
the washing of a windshield, the making of coffee,
the taking of a shower, or the reading of an email
is sacred.

All is sacred:
the simple, the glorious,
the disgusting, the beautiful.

They proclaim a great truth within the mystery:

    This is.

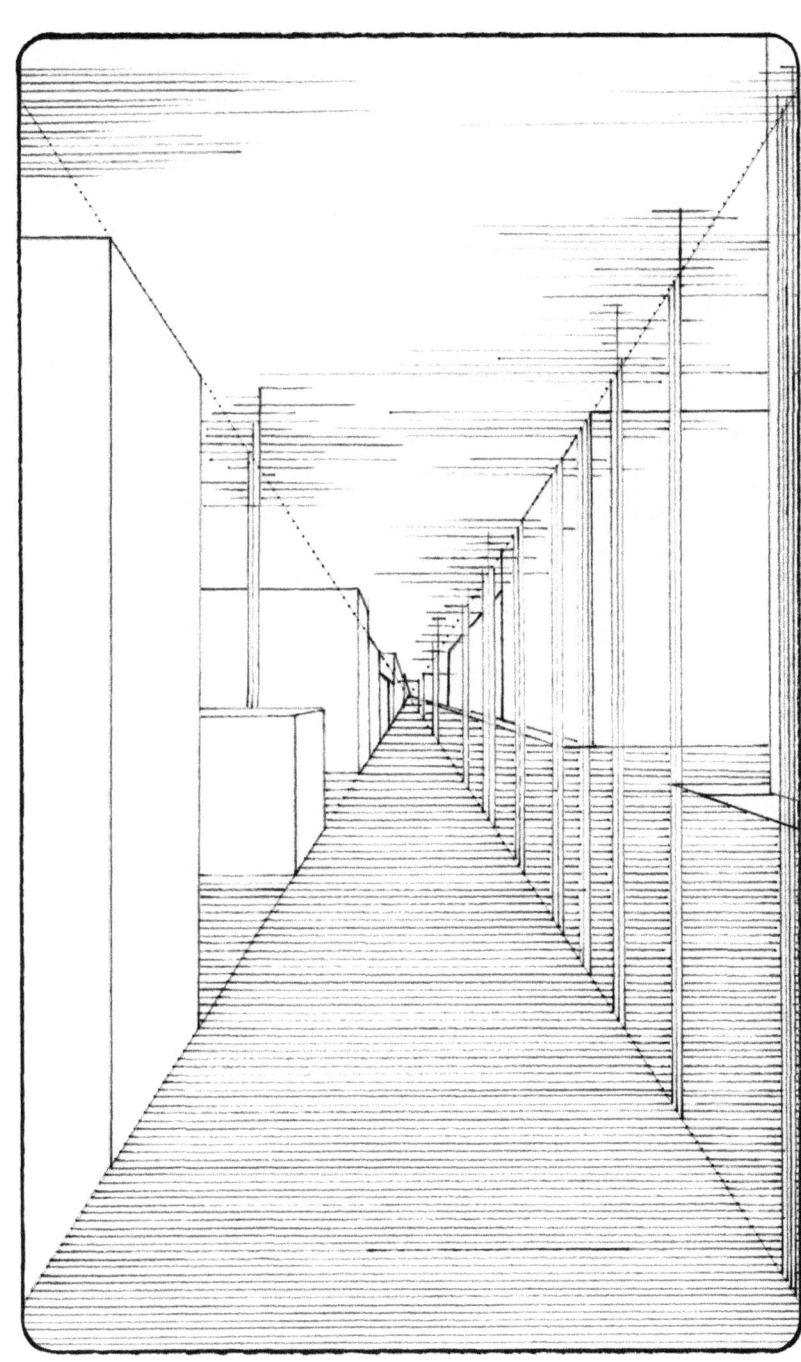

Awakened Abodes

The awakened abodes open naturally. There is no work to do, no book to read, and no teacher to find. Their opening is a remembering of what I already know to be true and certain, like a jewel resting in the palm of my own hand.

It happens in the precious brief moment when I see—when I really see—the string that's attached to every you and to every me: to every distant happening, to every wonderful moment that turned to something difficult, and to every sadness that was once at the start of every happiness.

That in this moment of seeing, my temptation to judge, compare, and define seems to fall away. Without effort, it just falls a w a y.

And I feel what the moment asks of me without the need to grasp or keep it, or to run or push it away. I am at peace with what is, and I find myself in the awakened abode of equanimity (upekkha).

And without trying, I'm filled with a sense of gratitude and goodwill towards all things. I fall in love with what is, and I find myself in the awakened abode of loving-kindness (metta).

And should my awakened and loving heart encounter suffering, I meet it without effort in the awakened abode of compassion (karuna).

And should my awakened and loving heart encounter the happiness and delight of others, I meet it without effort in the fourth abode of joy (mudita).

And from here, I begin to see that this once elusive state is actually everywhere I look: in every dance, in every Christmas tree ornament, in every silly joke, in every sparkle of delight that reminds me of what my heart already knows.

097 Armor

I wear my armor everywhere I go. I've been forging it since
I was a kid. I know when to talk and when to shut up.
I know my place. I know when to join in and attack, and
I know when to run away.

I keep it bright and shiny. I care about how I look (and I care
about how you look, too). I silently judge. I'm sarcastic and
sharp. I gossip. My life is amazing on social media, just
as my comments are thoughtful and witty (I know because
I see all the likes—I check frequently). I seldom really reveal
anything, or if I do, I couch it with some kind of escape
valve or self-deprecating humor. If I don't know you, I keep
conversation civil and unimportant, things like the weather
and sports (even though I don't care about sports).

I'm smart to wear my armor because life is not a nice
place. People will take advantage of you. People are
cruel. People are assholes. It's dog-eat-dog, there are
no free lunches, and everyone is out for themselves,
so why should I be any different? Just to get eaten alive?
No thanks.

But I can't see out of it, and everything sounds so dull
and echoey. It's hard to breathe in here, and it's so heavy
and rusted that I can hardly move. Come to think of it,
I'm not sure it protects me from getting hurt because
I'm hurting all the time. Shit, this isn't armor at all—it's
a prison! It's a death shroud! What's even worse is that
I'm so used to wearing it that it's become me now,
so much so that I don't even realize or remember
anymore that I'm the one who made it.

098 Blessings of the Three Foundations

May you Live Fully.
May you Love Freely.
May you Give Completely.

May you Live Fully.
> May you see the walls that you build around yourself
> clearly, and in doing so, may they crumble.

> May you be the person you most want to be.

May you Love Freely.
> May you find someone in your heart who you love without
> condition, and in knowing that this capacity for love lives
> within you, may you point it squarely at yourself.

> May you love everyone everywhere and everywhen
> without condition, removing all thought of good
> or bad, leaving only Love in your wake.

May you Give Completely.
> May you know that there is no separation between what
> is inside and what is outside—between what is self and
> what is other—and that in tending to ourselves, we are
> really tending to the world.

> May you know that even the tiniest step you take
> on your own journey doesn't just change you—
> it changes everything.

099 When in Doubt

When the mantras sound tuneless
When the sutras sound lifeless
When the gurus get arrested
When the old standbys lie down
When the therapists aren't accepting any new patients
When the magical whimsical waving dancing leaves
are just leaves
When the Buddhists forget who's Buddha
When this book is no refuge at all
When nothing else works
When all else fails:
Help someone.

It can be anyone:
    someone loved, someone at work, someone at school,
    someone anonymous, someone who doesn't need
    a lot, someone who needs everything, someone on the
    brink, someone who is mostly fine, someone who
    is great and deserves it, someone who is a complete
    jerk and doesn't. . .
Help them.
    Hold a door, pay a compliment, ask if they're OK, wash
    the dishes, dogsit, tell them their music is really cool and
    that they're brave for putting it out there.
And listen.
    Say things like "tell me more" or "say more about that"
    or "that sounds incredible" or "that must have been really
    hard" or "I'm so sorry that happened" or "Well, I happen
    to think you're great."

Try it as an experiment, and see what happens when you
have no more moves
to make and you. . .
Help someone.

The Immeasurable Vows of the Bodhisattva aren't reserved for anyone in particular. All one needs to do is say them.

Sentient beings are numberless.
I vow to liberate them.

Delusions are endless.
I vow to end them.

The ways of Compassion and Wisdom are boundless.
I vow to embody them.

The Way is unattainable.
I vow to attain it.

100 Attention

One day, as Master Ikkyu was seated in the garden composing a poem, a student approached with a question: "Master, can you please write something of great wisdom?"

Master Ikkyu dipped his brush in the ink and wrote:

Attention.

The student thought for a moment, and then asked, "Is that it? That's all?"

To which Master Ikkyu wrote:

Attention. Attention.

Clearly annoyed, the student huffed, "What is wise about this? There's nothing profound here!"

To which Master Ikkyu wrote:

Attention. Attention. Attention.

The student, now boiling over, cried out, "What does this word 'Attention' even mean?!"

Master Ikkyu replied gently, "Attention means attention."

101

Four-Year-Olds, Everyone

Picture every difficult person as a four-year-old kid:
 Every overbearing boss,
 Every unfair teacher,
 Every intimidating audience,
 Every judgmental parent,
 Every social media loudmouth,
 Every probably-soon-to-be-ex-friend,
 Every volume-cranked-to-eleven news pundit,
 Every the-sign-says-ten-items-or-less-but-that-guy-has-
 fifty-items guy,
 Every I'd-never-take-their-advice-in-a-million-years
 advice giver,
 Every whoever it is who you struggle with,
 including yourself—

Look at them.
Look at their face.
 You can see it, right?
 They're four years old.
 Even with that beard,
 Even with those lines,
 Even with that graying hair—
 Four years old.

See it?
 Maybe with a juice-stained mouth
 (and you know their hands are sticky),
 Maybe with hair sticking up everywhere,
 Maybe with a nose that's in a big need of a tissue.

Look! They're just a four-year-old kid.
 They don't have any power over anything real.
 They don't define anyone's life.

They're loud, sure, and I've got to deal with them (because they're not going to let me not deal with them, after all, they're four), but I'm not going to let a four-year-old kid take away my sense of identity.

I'm not going to let a four-year-old kid ruin my entire day (week, month, year, life).
I'm going to handle it as nicely as I can,
And then I'm going to move on.

They're OK.
I'm OK.

Until the next four-year-old kid comes along (which is likely any moment now).

102

Reflection

What does a mirror's image capture?
Lines revealing wisdom or regret?
Features inspiring gratitude or disgust?
An aura of possibility or a grip of resignation?
Does the mirror reflect what's true,

Or is it like trying to capture the wind in a plastic bag,
Or a stream in a bucket?
—Inadequate—

Reflecting none of the movement and current,
None of the cause and impact,
None of the beauty and majesty,
None of the astonishing truth,
None of who is truly there.

103 A Place, A Visit, A Word, A Gift

Search your heart for a place of rest and peace and lightness and ease, a place of love, safety, and warmth:

    A firepit on a cool autumn night.

    A quiet beach.

    A forest path lined with sweet honeysuckle.

    A bench along a flowing river.

Have a seat. Rest and receive every bit of it. Take in the sounds and scents. Feel the air.

Someone unexpected and wonderful comes and sits next to you, and your heart is instantly filled to overflowing.

    Maybe it's an old friend, or a family member, or a friend long passed. Maybe it's an animal whose warm head you haven't pet in far too long. Their love for you is without condition and you are wrapped completely in it. Allow yourself to feel every measure as they reach over and touch your arm. For a moment or two, allow yourself to simply be with them.

Now they lean over and whisper something in your ear.

    Something that will help you along your path. Something for you to remember in times that are dark, or sorrowful, or times when you think all may be lost. It's only a word or maybe a sentence, but somehow it's perfect. Somehow it's exactly what you need to hear.

    What do they tell you?

They have a gift for you.

    A small token to help you be exactly you in all of the most wonderful ways—kind, hopeful, joyful, grateful, compassionate, courageous, and loving.

    What is it? What did they give you?

With deep gratitude, you hold it in your hands.
    What does this gift mean to you? If you are not sure, you
    can ask them—they'll tell you.
    What does it mean?

Sit together for a few more moments, or as long as you want.
    Know that this is with you now and always will be:
    Whenever you want, or whenever you need, you can visit
    this place, this friend, these words, and this gift.

They are always with you.
They are within you and always will be.

Turning Maslow on His Head

Published in 1943, Abraham Maslow's Hierarchy of Needs is widely taught as a basis for human motivation.

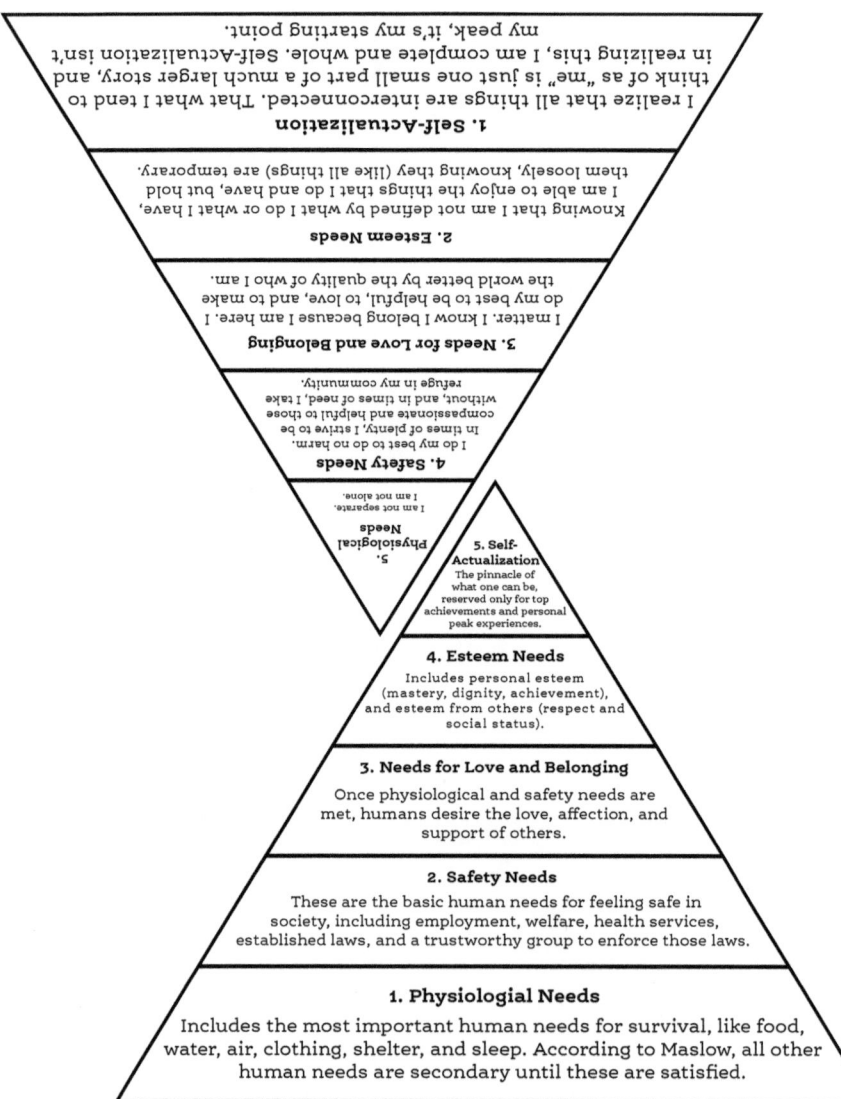

1. Self-Actualization
I realize that all things are interconnected. That what I tend to think of as "me" is just one small part of a much larger story, and in realizing this, I am complete and whole. Self-Actualization isn't my peak, it's my starting point.

2. Esteem Needs
Knowing that I am not defined by what I do or what I have, I am able to enjoy the things that I do and have, but hold them loosely, knowing they (like all things) are temporary.

3. Needs for Love and Belonging
I matter. I know I belong because I am here. I do my best to be helpful, to love, and to make the world better by the quality of who I am.

4. Safety Needs
I do my best to do no harm. In times of plenty, I strive to be compassionate and helpful to those without, and in times of need, I take refuge in my community.

5. Physiological Needs
I am not separate. I am not alone.

5. Self-Actualization
The pinnacle of what one can be, reserved only for top achievements and personal peak experiences.

4. Esteem Needs
Includes personal esteem (mastery, dignity, achievement), and esteem from others (respect and social status).

3. Needs for Love and Belonging
Once physiological and safety needs are met, humans desire the love, affection, and support of others.

2. Safety Needs
These are the basic human needs for feeling safe in society, including employment, welfare, health services, established laws, and a trustworthy group to enforce those laws.

1. Physiologial Needs
Includes the most important human needs for survival, like food, water, air, clothing, shelter, and sleep. According to Maslow, all other human needs are secondary until these are satisfied.

The Water Mirror

Once upon a time, long ago, in an old home of wood and stone, there lived a set of twin sisters. Identical in their beauty alone, one sister was warm, carefree, and joyful, while the other was dreary, somber, and brooding, and whenever they visited the nearby village, they would be greeted in kind. The first sister would be warmly welcomed and well-wished, while the other would be coldly met with averted gazes and downturned eyes. Soon, the brooding sister came to find the stubborn roots of jealousy and hatred tangling themselves around her heart.

Consumed with desire to be adored, the envious sister hatched a plan to win the villagers' love over her sister. After readying herself in the bowl of water they used as their morning mirror, she clouded the mirror's waters with dyes of green and crimson, turmeric, and lac. With wicked glee, she thrilled at the thought of her sister being unable to match her beauty, only to find her twin playfully splashing the colored water and dancing her way through the door and onto the road toward the town, where she was yet again met with warmth and affection.

The following morning, filled with hate and loathing, she moved the mirror bowl next to the morning's roaring fire, causing its waters to boil and bubble over. Her heart pounded with excitement as she imagined the inevitable comparisons between her own carefully crafted beauty against her sister's two days' worth of unwashed and unfixed features, but was again dumbfounded to discover no change in the greetings of the townspeople.

Having given up, she found herself lethargic, listless, and lifeless. Alone in her torpor, she refused to move for many days, despite her sister's caring invitations to meet the wonder of the world outside. As time sung its melody, the waters of the mirror began to grow green with algae and then with moss, and she languished alone for days upon days. As the weeks passed, her dimmed spirit transformed from weariness into worry. She questioned if she could ever be loved by anyone, and as though drowning, her mind

thrashed and clawed for any idea that might release her
from her anxious suffering. Hoping that the wind might
carry her worries far away, she opened every window,
pleading with the air to cleanse her of her dread. Rushing
to her mirror, she watched as the algae and slime was
pushed over the bowl's edge, but instead of being greeted
by the return of her own beauty, she was met only by
the ripples and waves on the mirror's surface, and she
doubted if she had ever been beautiful. In fact, she became
quite certain that she had not, and as she plummeted
into despair, she tearfully collected handfuls of dirt and
soil, plunging them into the mirror's water and violently
splashing until only a brown shadow could be found.

     She had exhausted all she had and all she believed
she was, and she began to cry in abject resignation, covering
her face with her hands to hide her tears only to feel the
warm touch of her sister's hand on her wrist, pulling her
from her seat and guiding her to the water mirror. As she
approached, she saw that the silt she had mixed earlier had
separated from the water on its own and now rested at the
bottom of the bowl, revealing a crystal-clear reflection of
the full moon coming through the window. The image was
so bright and beautiful and lifelike that she touched the
water as if to caress the moon's face and in doing so, gasped
in surprise when the image waved. Her startle broke the
reflection's spell, and she turned her eyes upward, where
through the window she saw the moon as though for the
first time. The moon seemed illuminated from within, and
overcome by it, she felt her own living force as the moon's
living force, her breath as the moon's breath, all her joys as
the moon's joys, and all her sorrows as the moon's sorrows.
She felt the moon's light fill her to fullness and realized
that she was lacking for nothing—that she was whole and
complete—and effortlessly, she felt love shine from within
her for the moon and everything under its gaze: for all of the
townspeople, for all manner of creatures everywhere, for her
sister, and for herself.

Note from the Desert

To whatever poor wretched soul finds this note:

I thought I was safe and had it all figured out. I didn't see this coming and damned if I can find a drop of water anywhere. I'm dying. Things that once did the trick just don't do the trick anymore. I don't feel like I've stepped off the path as much as I feel like there may not have ever been a path to begin with. I'm lost. I'm utterly lost.

In what seems like my last moments here, I'm thinking about my wonderful kid, my sunshine who knows who they are better than I ever did (even though I don't think they know it). I'm thinking about my wife who makes me laugh so hard and will listen to me drone on about anything. I'm thinking about laughing with her. I'm thinking about my tiny little dog who sleeps when she wants and plays when she wants and doesn't seem to get too bothered in between. I'm thinking about how she'll let you kiss her head, no matter how much she just wants to sleep. I'm thinking about my best friends and how I wish my heart was half as big as theirs. I'm thinking about how I'm glad that I get to breathe and get to look around and listen. Funny, the leaves are still falling—I think they were already all gone by this time last year. The sky is so blue behind them. The birds are so busy!

If I ever make it out of here, I have to remember—
    Notice what's right in front of you.
    Love and don't hide it.
    Help without a thought of anything in return.
    Forgive.

Put this note somewhere safe. Keep it close by, because I have a bad feeling that this won't be the only time this happens—that the floor falls right out from under you. When it happens, please don't forget this:

No matter what, you're OK.

Your friend always,
You

The Sun Is Always Rising

In the event that
everything goes just as you hoped it would,
> May you enjoy it fully, may it fill your heart and radiate
> outward from you.
> May you be proud of your great effort and care, knowing
> that effort and care is how intent shows itself.
> May you be grateful for the opportunity, knowing its
> rarity and recognizing all of the efforts of others who
> helped to bring it to life.
> May you be humble and gracious, knowing that one's win
> is often another's loss.

In the event that
everything doesn't go just as you hoped it would,
> May you know deeply that who you are can never
> be diminished.
> May you take care of your heart, being mindful of the
> stories that disappointment can create.
> May your thoughts be clear.
> May you take refuge in knowing that the most wonderful
> things in life include disappointments in their paths,
> even though the preciousness of what's to come
> can be veiled.

May you always be exactly who you are,
no matter what you do or don't do,
no matter what you have or don't have.
May you know how much you are loved.

May your story bow to every turn within it,
knowing that the greatest tales require every chapter.

May your story be sung by the wind and the trees and
the lessons of your life be passed forward in the insistent
chirps of hummingbirds and the tireless bleats of crickets.

May your story set into motion life's sweetest beauty, becoming some great future mystery as to how it all came to be as wonderful as it is.

May you come to see that the sun is always rising.

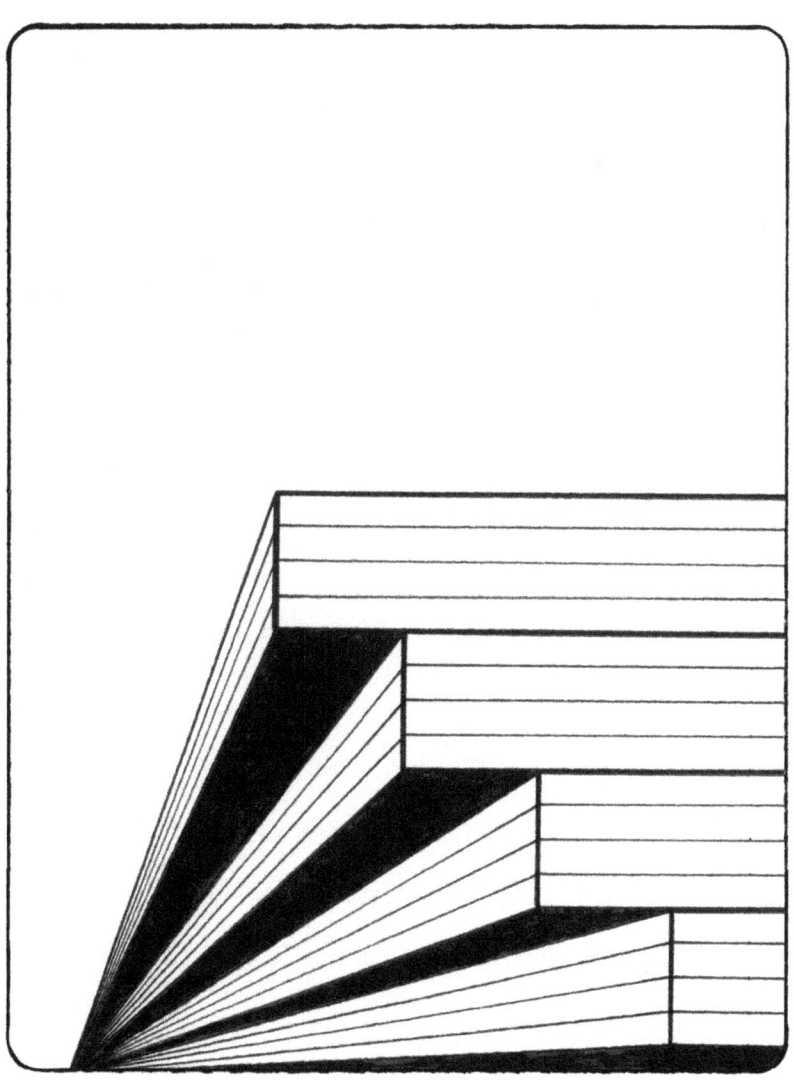

108 Reminders

I keep a list of quotes, lessons, stories, and thoughts on my phone. Being the incredibly creative guy that I am, I named the file, "Reminders," because that is exactly what they are. When I'm stuck or spiraling (or spiraled?) and I can't remember what good days look or feel like, I bring up my phone (it's usually not very far away), and I read them. I keep the file short—no longer than a couple of pages, if I were to print it out, because when I'm in trouble, I can't afford to go looking through the weeds, I need something that hits me right in the chest and pulls me out (or at least grabs me by the shoulders and turns me ever so slightly in a new direction).

This book was born from that list. In working to help other people, I found that they always had the answer within them already, they just forgot where they put it.

So . . .

Create your own list of reminders (you can even call it, "Reminders" if you want—I promise I won't chase after you for copyright infringement.)

Open a note on your phone or create a document, or . . . go buy a tiny notebook that can fit in your pocket (they still sell those, I think), and write what works. Write what inspires you. Include movie quotes if that does the trick. Include poems, song lyrics, sayings from the Buddha, Jesus, or Nicolas Cage—whatever works!

Keep it with you. Open it daily to remind yourself of who you are, so that when you're not feeling much like yourself, you have signposts of your own making pointing your way back.

Keep it short. Keep it powerful—only the best stuff makes the cut. Don't be afraid to edit it so that it is always what you need to read most (I edit mine all the time).

May you be free from suffering and the causes of suffering.
May you be healthy.
May you know peace and lightness and ease.
May you be free to choose how you experience the world.
May you be the person you choose to be.

May you be free.

_/_

Fingers Pointing to the Moon

"What is most personal is most universal."
—Carl R. Rogers

———————————

I am an ordained Buddhist priest (an Oshō in my tradition). I teach mindfulness to individuals and organizations, and I work as an integrative group facilitator for an intensive outpatient program for both adolescents and adults. I have had the honor of working with people from all backgrounds and spiritual traditions on everything from career challenges to crises of faith, from questions of identity to questions of worth, from spiraling marriages to spiraling mental illnesses, and from the despair of losing a loved one to the fragile acceptance of one's own impending death.

Throughout, I realized—over and over again—that the most powerful, helpful, and transformative wisdom was never anything I said or did, but rather something that the person held within their heart already—they just needed to be reminded of it. What's more, I continue to find this to be true for myself. Every time I struggle to find peace in my own life, what ultimately pulls me out is never some new information or insight, but rather something I already hold within my heart—I just need to rekindle, rediscover, or remember it. I just need to wake it up.

With this in mind, my sincere hope with **refuge in small things** is that something in these 108 Buddhist lessons, fables, stories, and personal reflections (potholes, dead-ends, stumbles, and all) might serve—as the Zen folks say—as "fingers pointing to the moon." In other words, that they might point you to something true and alive within yourself, helping to free you from suffering, to feel more worthy, to live more fully, and to love more deeply.

Instead of being a book about Buddhism, **refuge in small things** is therefore intended to be a book of practice, and for this reason I thought it might be helpful to include some notes of background, explanation, and/or recommendations for further exploration where it seemed appropriate or interesting to do so. These notes also give me an opportunity to thank some of the teachers, friends, and influential authors for their generous wisdom, support, inspiration, and love. Thank you all so very much, I'm deeply grateful.

—Mike Travisano

For more information about Mike, visit www.theartofmondaymorning.com.

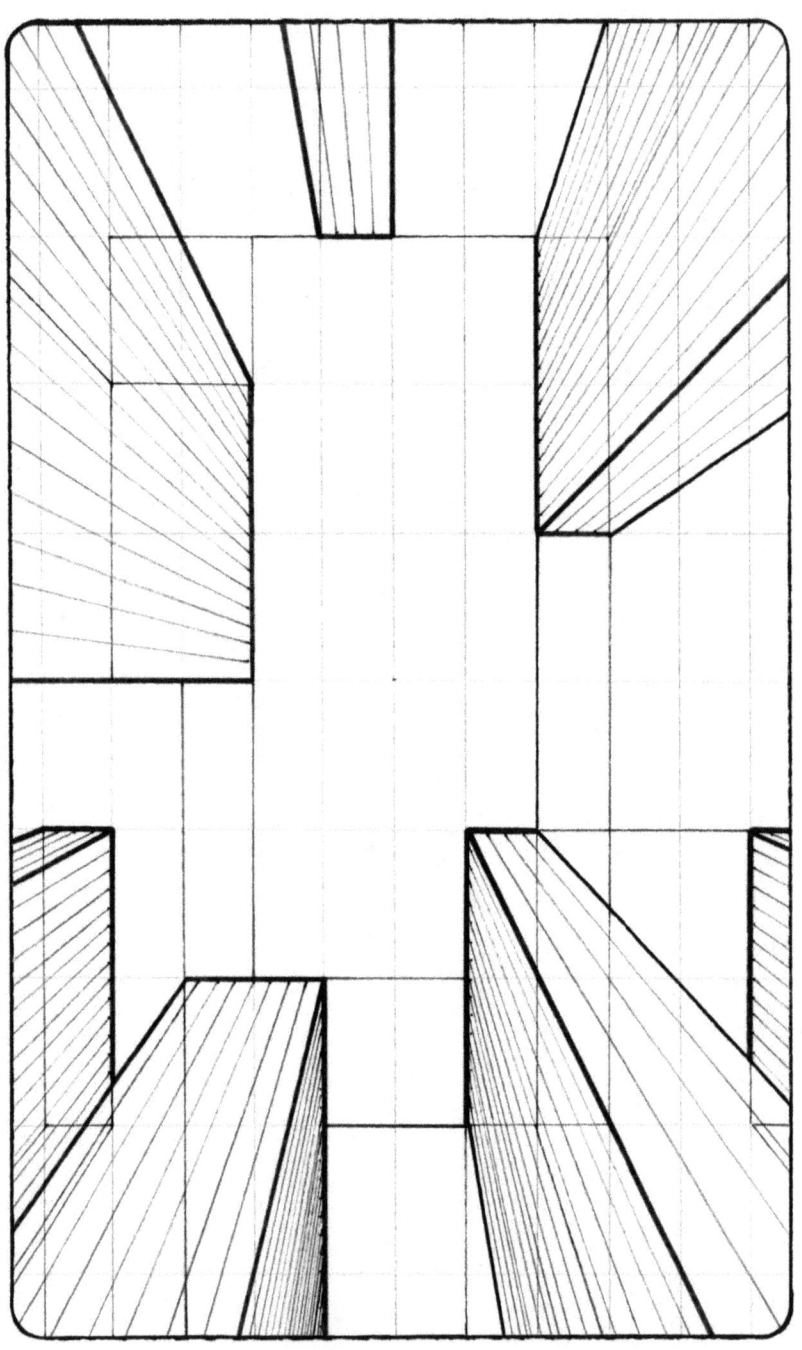

About the images

"Space is essentially a mental construct.
We imagine space to be there, even if we experience it as a void,
an absence we cannot perceive."
—Lebbeus Woods

My drawings are thoughts about space made visual—like annotations. But space cannot be literally captured on paper, it is an act of representation and needs our perception and perspective. We inhabit space, interact with it constantly (consciously and subconsciously), and yet we bring our whole understanding of life with us in our perspective. We each see space differently. Drawings are our notes about our experience, about our life, about our feelings, and about our being.

I've tried to pair my understanding of these entries—my felt sense of them—with drawings that have a similar action or feeling or presence, but of course my perception and understanding of these marks will differ from yours. I hope they allow time for your mind to pause and give your eye a place to rest while your thoughts linger on the entries, adding another sense to engage in the understanding of these stories, lessons, parables, and reflections.

—Jess Gibson
  (Rise & Render)

For more information about Jess, visit www.riseandrender.com.

001   The Prison is Locked from the Inside

002   The Practice of Enlightenment

003   A Lamp Unto Myself
Both quotes in this entry are from the *Maha-parinibbana Sutta*, which tells of the final days of the Buddha. If you'd like to explore this sutra, as well as others referenced in this book, *accesstoinsight.org* and *dhammatalks.org* are both wonderful online resources for classical translations of the Buddha's teachings.

004   Mindfulness 101
Much of the way I present the practice of mindfulness in *refuge in small things* is grounded in the work of my friend and teacher, The RT Rev. Dr. Anthony Stultz, who created a practical system for self-inquiry that is not only deeply rooted in the dharma, but is also accessible, practical in a modern context, and profoundly liberating. For more information on this approach, I highly recommend his book, *Free Your Mind: The Four Directions System of Mindfulness* or visit *asksenseitony.com*. Gassho, Sensei.

005   Me as a Matter of Perspective

006   The Tree

007   refuge in small things

008   Kanzeon

009   The Vast Net of Indra
The quote in this entry is from the Flower-Garland Sutra (*Avatamsaka Sutra*), which is believed to have been compiled several hundred years after the death of the Buddha. While it covers several Buddhist topics, I find its descriptions of interdependency to be absolutely beautiful. Various versions are available to read online. I recommend a very comfortable chair (it's very long), and maybe some Pink Floyd (it's very colorful).

010   Feeding the Hungry Ghosts
In many Buddhist traditions, Hungry Ghosts (*gaki*, in Japanese) represent aspects within ourselves that haunt us. They may be ruminating thoughts about past actions, worries for the future, or any number of ways in which we are troubled by the difficulties and challenges in our lives. In the Buddhist community in which I am a part (and in others worldwide), we celebrate the "Feeding of the Hungry Ghosts" annually by welcoming these aspects to reveal themselves, and by feeding them with wisdom and compassion. In our ceremony, we write down something that has been "haunting" us on a small piece of paper, and then burn the paper in a *goma*, or ceremonial fire, symbolically releasing ourselves from its influence, or *karma*.

011   The Supreme Meal
Roshi Bernie Glassman wrote beautifully about making the Supreme Meal in his book *Instructions to the Cook*. In it, he writes about the work that he and his Zen community did to establish organizations in New York City to employ, feed, and house people who were otherwise thought of as being beyond employment, beyond help, and beyond worth. One memorable example is the Greyston Bakery, which grew from a small kitchen making and delivering homemade desserts locally to an industrial enterprise supplying Ben and Jerry's with brownies for their ice cream sandwiches—all the while staffed with people who

had served long prison sentences, people living with addictions, and people without homes.

012 Love as a Round Trip

This is my version of a loving-kindness, or metta, meditation. There are many wonderful resources for further exploration of this type of meditation, with one of my favorites being author and teacher Sharon Salzberg, who offers books and instruction on the subject.

013 One Day

014 A Middle Way

This retelling of Siddhartha Gautama's journey paralleled with a modern take, with all of the struggle, self-doubt, and redirection therein, is intended to reinforce a notion that I find particularly powerful: The most special thing about the Buddha is that he wasn't special at all. He was a person just like you and me, and that the capacity to find peace within ourselves exists in every heart, no matter what we've experienced or done.

015 The Great Battle

The broad strokes of my retelling of the Buddha's awakening come from The Buddhacharita, an epic poem attributed to Asvaghosa around the 2nd century CE. One element from Asvaghosa's version that I didn't include but find fascinating and beautiful is Siddhartha's encounter with the Naga King—the great serpent. In many Buddhist traditions, the Naga are wise protectors and teachers. In The Buddhacharita, the Naga King blesses Siddharthatha as he approaches the tree of his awakening, and in others, he wraps himself around Siddhartha and opens his hood above him to keep him dry as he meditates in the rain.

016 The Buddha's Four Noble Truths

Like tofu or a fine risotto, Buddhism took on the flavors of the cultures it encountered as it spread from northern India to the greater world. This is why Tibetan practices, icons, and styles look so different from Southeast Asian practices, or Zen in Japan, or modern practices in the West. One foundation that they all share, though, is the Four Noble Truths. Classically, the Buddha offers this teaching in what is known as the Dhammacakkappavattana Sutta, which is often referred to as "the turning of the Dharma wheel" or "setting the wheel of the Dharma in motion."

017 Both/And (a view from the path of understanding)

This entry, as well as the subsequent seven entries, attempt to illustrate a modern, pragmatic view of each part of the Buddha's Noble Eightfold Path. I again recommend accesstoinsight.org and dhammatalks.org for readers who wish to explore the Buddha's classical teachings on these eight as depicted in the sutras. A good starting point being the Saccavibhanga Sutta, which encapsulates the Buddha's teachings for all eight aspects of the path.

018 (on the path of) Intent

019 Finding the Person Under the Suffering (on the path of speech)

020 The Psycle of Rebirth (on the path of action)

021 Work/Life Balance (on the path of livelihood)

022   Feeding the Wolf (on the path of effort)
I've attributed the source of the good wolf/bad wolf parable as being an indigenous American folktale, but many versions exist with attributions to other cultures. The version presented here is as it was first introduced to me.

023   hmm. (on the path of concentration)

024   This for That (on the path of mindfulness)

025   Well, Is It?

026   Teachers

027   The Arrows of Pain and Suffering
The Buddha's original teaching on these arrows can be found in the *Sallatha Sutta*.

028   One Coin, Two Sides
I have found in working with others that, very often, the amount of one's suffering—once transformed—often pales in comparison to the amount of compassion that they are able to realize in their own hearts and towards the hearts of others. The intimate relationship they have with their own suffering allows them to instantly recognize it in others—in micro expressions, in actions, in postures, in words, etc.—and to be able to respond to it immediately and without judgment or doubt. In lighter moments, I think of it as "the world's most hard-earned superpower."

029   Compassion Is an Action

030   Nothing Is Never Not a Beginning
Thank you, Mom, for your blessing to include this one. I love you very much.

031   Is That So?
Hakuin was a Zen priest and teacher who lived in Japan in the 17th and 18th centuries, and who is considered a legendary figure. The tale presented here is my spiced-up version of one of his most famous anecdotes. For a more traditional telling of this tale, as well as other "Zen fables," readers may wish to check out *Zen Flesh, Zen Bones: A Collection of Zen and Pre-Zen Writings* by Paul Reps and Nyogen Senzaki.

032   The Flower
A deep bow to the late Thich Nhat Hahn, who coined the word "interbeing," and whose wonderful books and life inspired this entry.

033   Light as a Feather

034   Bob's Tattoos
The single most common question I received from readers of early versions of this book was, "Is Bob real?" I am very happy to report that not only is Bob quite real, but these are his words. With his permission, I merely changed this entry from his first-person account to the one included here. Bob lives and works as a grief counselor and purpose guide in Saint Simons, Georgia. For more information about my very good pal, Bob, visit soularborist.com.

035   _/_
The "prayer hands" symbol for which this piece is titled represents the *gassho*, which is a symbol of profound gratitude and deep respect. In the gesture of a gassho, the left hand represents the Ego Self, and the right

hand represents the True Self. In bringing them together, we proclaim that they are not separate, but rather they are one.

036   The Three Tenets

037   Great Doubt

038   Great Faith

039   Great Courage
In some Zen traditions, this idea is also known as "Great Determination."

040   Roar

041   Make Tea
This is my retelling of a famous Japanese folktale.

042   The Eight Worldly Winds
The original teaching of the Buddha upon which this entry is based is the Loka-vipatti Sutta.

043   Humility

044   The Holy Light Switch
The source of this quote from the Buddha is the Okkha Sutta.

045   Butsudan
This entry describes my own personal home altar, but I encourage readers to consider creating a physical space of your own—a picture, a candle, a flower, an object, etc.—something that touches the sacred within your heart the moment you see it. It need not be big, ornate, or even obvious, but having something like this can be a powerful tool to remind us of what is most important within us when the thoughts in our heads threaten to steer us away from ourselves.

046   The Elephant in the Room
Every word of this story is true, and there is very little in my life that hasn't been positively shaped in some way by my teacher, mentor, and cherished friend, Joe Brtalik. Without him, I don't believe I'd be a Buddhist priest today, and I'm not exactly sure that I'd still be alive. While not expressly Buddhist, Joe's training under Peter Senge and Fred Kofman from the MIT Sloan School of Business and the Center for Organizational Learning is the path that intersected with mine in that conference room at IBM in the year 2000. A deep, deep bow of gratitude to you, Joe. Thank you for opening your hand to me for all these years.

047   An Email from a Very Old Ancestor
This entry was chiefly inspired by the work of author and psychologist, Dr. Rick Hanson, who writes beautifully about the science of the brain and well-being. Among his books, I highly recommend Buddha's Brain and Hardwiring Happiness (but they're all terrific).

048   Let Life Live You

049   Maybe
This Chinese parable, commonly known as "The Parable of the Farmer," is from the Taoist tradition and dates to the 2nd century BCE.

050   Herding Cats

054   Crash Course
This parable is famous in many Buddhist traditions, and is commonly referred to as "The Empty Boat."

056   This Because That
My very deepest love and gratitude to my wife, to our wonderful child, to the Bodhisattvas disguised as our dogs, and to the millions of laughs and countless moments of support. Thank you for being everything that glows brightest in my chest today.

061   Energy & Perseverance (*Virya*)
In some traditions, this paramita is also taught as diligence of practice. Like the teaching of right effort, I find this particularly helpful, because for many years, I imagined that if I just read the right stuff or found the right teacher, I might someday become enlightened and never suffer again, but then I started to notice words within the dharma like perseverance, effort, and diligence, and a wonderful light bulb turned on: It isn't about walking somewhere—it's about walking.

063   Wisdom (*Prajna*)
One of the most important texts in Mahayana Buddhism (the branch of Buddhism from which my own tradition stems) is the Heart Sutra (the Prajna Paramita), which teaches the wisdom of emptiness, or shunyata: that nothing exists in and of itself. This work includes the very famous line, "Form is emptiness and emptiness is form," from which I've liberally modeled this entry. The Heart Sutra also ends with "the spell uttered" by the Bodhisattva of Compassion, Avalokiteshwara, who chants the mantra, "Gate, Gate, Paragate, Parasamgate, Bodhi Svaha!" ("Gone, Gone, Gone to the other shore, Gone completely to the other shore, Awake Ah!"—the "other shore" being a metaphor for enlightenment.)

066   What Happens When You Die?
Even though Buddhism originated during a time in India when beliefs of reincarnation were widespread, the Buddha famously refused to answer questions like the one posed in this entry. In the Aggi-Vacchagotta Sutta, the Buddha is questioned on a number of metaphysical topics, such as "Does an enlightened being exist after death?" and "Are the soul and the body the

same?" To each of these questions, the Buddha replies that any position or conventional answer is merely a "clinging of the mind" that only serves to cause suffering and distract us from the more important task at hand, which is (referring back to the Four Noble Truths) to realize that ending our suffering is not about satiating the things for which we thirst (like knowing whether or not we survive physical death), but rather by ending the thirst, itself. In this way, Buddhism is unique among the major spiritual traditions— it doesn't answer questions like this one, but rather allows the mystery to be. In my own practice, I have found great refuge in leaning hard into this spaciousness.

067   Pulling the Rug Out from Under Myself
In challenging the idea of a permanent self, the Buddha taught that what I tend to perceive as a single, unchanging "me" is really made of five interconnecting and ever-changing aggregates, or "heaps" (skandhas). This entry attempts to look under the hood of these five. The original teaching of the Buddha on these aggregates is the Kandha Sutta, with the Buddha's challenge to our notion of a permanent self presented in the Anatta-lakkhana Sutta.

068   Judgment

069   Rock-Bottomless

070   Milarepa's Guests
In Tibetan culture, Milarepa is a highly honored and celebrated figure. Believed to have lived during the 11th century, there are many colorful tales about his life, with the folktale on which this is based being one of the more famous ones.

071   Icons, Not Idols
I think that it's worth noting that a common metaphor for Zen practice is "polishing the mirror."

072   Thought Experiment

073   Weighing What Matters

074   Origin Story
My first introduction to the idea of "me" as being an expression of all there is came from the writings of Alan Watts. By virtue of the hard work of his son, Mark Watts, Alan Watts continues to be a fantastic gateway for further exploration into eastern traditions and philosophies. I strongly recommend to anyone that they explore Alan Watts' incredibly thought-provoking (and entertaining) recordings and books. I'm not sure I can pick just one, but The Wisdom of Insecurity as well as a collection of his talks, Out of Your Mind, are the two I revisit most frequently. Visit alanwatts.org for more information.

075   Julia

076   Five Little Things to Remember
The classical text from which this entry on the "five remembrances" draws is the Upajjhatthana Sutta.

077   How, Not What

078   A Heavy Load
Another famous parable from the Zen tradition.

079   Jizo

082   The Genjokoan of the Turtles

Life has a way of presenting the same difficult situation over and over until we've learned what it is asking of us. In some Zen traditions, this is known as a genjokoan.

083   The Wisdom in Our Challenges

A fable from the Zen tradition.

084   Everyone Buddha

085   A Glimpse of Enlightenment

Other joke candidates for this entry included: I bought the world's worst thesaurus. Not only is it terrible, but it's also terrible; and Why do you never see hippos hiding in trees? Because they're so good at it.

086   House on Fire

This entry owes a great deal to the work of Dr. Richard Schwartz and his Internal Family Systems (IFS) model. IFS suggests that as we grow and encounter challenges, we develop parts within ourselves that act as protectors. For example, if I encounter a bully in the third-grade, I may develop a part within my psyche that will work to keep me safe and make sure that I never go through that kind of difficult experience again: It will help me avoid bullies, avoid drinking fountains where bullies may congregate, avoid experiences where I may be emotionally exposed, etc. As I grow older, though, this part may continue to play this role, but instead of bullies at water fountains, it may be job interviews, asking people out on dates, or any situation where that part may perceive my heart to be at risk in the same way I experienced as a kid. In other words, I'll start to see water fountain bullies everywhere! Consequently, the urgency of these parts to keep me safe can result in inner voices that are critical, judgmental, and even harmful, and their advice can be unclear and unhelpful, because even though I may be decades older, that part still sees me as the kid at the water fountain. I'm an enormous fan of the IFS model because of how it proposes we relate to these parts within us. As revealed in this entry, my default mode is to desperately want my critical inner voices to go away. I may even vehemently hate them (and myself for having them), but if I can see that these voices are just aspects within myself that are trying to keep me safe (regardless of the poor quality of advice they may be offering), then I don't have to live with an inner enemy anymore. In fact, I can thank that inner voice. I can appreciate the burden they've carried, and I can suggest to them that they need not carry it alone any further—that they can rest, ride shotgun, and let a wiser me drive for a while. I hope my summary here is helpful, but I recommend researching the topic further. The IFS model is very popular these days in psychotherapeutic circles, but there are also wonderful mass-market resources as well, such as Dr. Schwartz' own books, No Bad Parts and You Are The One You've Been Waiting For. I also highly recommend Tim Ferriss' podcast interview with Dr. Schwartz (episode 492) of The Tim Ferriss Show for a live demonstration of how Dr. Schwartz utilizes the model in a therapeutic setting.

Also, a few words about the line in the entry about me being a "fully-ordained Buddhist priest who should be able to simply raise a flower to these thoughts and have them smile back at me." This is a reference to a famous story about a large group of people gathered to hear the Buddha teach, but instead of talking, the Buddha silently holds up a flower. While everyone else was baffled, Mahakasyapa, alone—awakened by the gesture—smiled. In the Chan and Zen traditions, this story is presented as a kōan, or "case for investigation," in a collection known as *The Gateless Gate*. Kōan practice is a cornerstone of Chan and Zen practice, but translations of these ancient Chinese cases can sometimes be impenetrable—but not Guo Gu's 2016 translation and commentary, *Passing Through The Gateless Barrier*. It is warm and funny and welcoming and so very insightful. I not only recommend it, but deeply thank Guo Gu for writing it. Guo Gu even makes the title, *Gateless Gate*, accessible, inviting us to see our problems, hang-ups, tragedies, etc.—our "gates" (or "barriers")—as the paths themselves for our own awakening, and in doing so, help us to see that there was never a barrier to begin with. May we come to see that our problems are "gateless." This is especially pertinent to my difficulty with the internet troll in this entry, as it was their obscene disruption that directly led to my own new relationship with my inner voice, the lessons that came from it that I've shared with my community and clients, and even any insight that you may get from it in this very book! So for this: a deep bow of gratitude to you, internet troll, wherever you are. Gassho. May you and your "hammercock" be free from suffering and the causes of suffering.

087   Finding an Inner Voice That's True

088   Taking In & Sending Out
This meditation is more commonly known as *tonglen* in Tibetan Buddhist traditions. My very first introduction to the practice was in Pema Chodron's beautiful book, *Start Where You Are*, which along with all her other work, I can't recommend highly enough.

089   Prayer Wheel

090   Fudo

091   The Thought Is Not the Thing

092   Words
Like "The Thought Is Not the Thing," this entry is attempting to lean very hard into the wisdom of what has famously become known as "the four statements of Zen," which describe Zen as:

> A special transmission outside of scripture,
> Beyond letters and words
> Pointing directly to one's True Nature,
> Awakening and becoming Buddha.

093   Bob and Weave

094   Breathe and Become
This entry is my take on a guided visualization that Jack Kornfield presents in his book, *The Wise Heart: A Guide to the Universal Teachings of Buddhist Psychology*. In addition to finding it helpful for myself, I've found this meditation to be very useful to others who are in the midst of confronting something challenging, be it awaiting the results of a biopsy or awaiting the results of a judge's sentencing. It's a beautiful reminder that the power and grace of our most treasured angels, bodhisattvas, and heroes is something that's available to us whenever we may need to call upon it.

095 Instructions to the Chief Cook

The 1,000-year-old set of instructions this entry references is a 12th century work called *Regulations for Zen Monasteries*, which was authored by the founder of the Soto school of Zen, Dogen Zenji. Based on an earlier Chinese work, Dogen outlines the proper method and character for one taking up the position of chief cook, or *tenzo*, for a traditional Zen monastery, emphasizing both the practical requirements for preparing meals for monks in residence, as well as the transformative aspects that are inherent in truly mindful cooking.

096 Awakened Abodes

The "Four Awakened Abodes," also known as "The Immeasurables" and "The Exalted Dwellings," are taught by the Buddha in a very famous sutra known as the *Kalama Sutta*, or "The Instructions to the Kalamas." In this sutra, the Buddha is questioned by a group of skeptical searchers who wonder why they should believe him. Famously, the Buddha advises that they should not believe him—or any other sage, teacher, writing, etc.—but rather they should only accept as true those things which they conclude for themselves to be true after their own thorough examination and testing. The Buddha further teaches that, if they are successful in this, then they will dwell in the exalted and boundless states of equanimity, loving-kindness, compassion, and sympathetic joy.

097 Armor

I would be remiss if I didn't reference here the work of Brené Brown, who has so reshaped the way so many of us understand shame and the power of vulnerability. I highly recommend her TEDx Houston talk on YouTube, "The Power of Vulnerability," as well as all her subsequent books, talks, and projects.

098 Blessings of the Three Foundations

In the Buddhist community in which I am a part, we traditionally offer this blessing annually as the first Dharma talk of the New Year. During this time, we also celebrate *Bonenkai*, where we mindfully choose to "forget the past year," and *Joya no Kane*, which is a Japanese Buddhist tradition of ringing a bell 108 times to cleanse past harmful actions and the impacts from them (*karma*). The number 108 represents the number of ways in which delusions are manifested, which is mathematically:

the six senses as understood in Buddhist traditions
(sight, hearing, touch, taste, smell, and mind)
x
the three ways I process time (past, present, and future)
x
the three ways I relate to my experiences (like, dislike, indifference)
x
the two conditions of intent (pure or impure)
= 108

099 When in Doubt

100 Attention

The figure in this parable, Ikkyū Sōjun, was a real-life 15th-century Zen master whose legendary (if not eccentric) nature precedes him. "Crazy Cloud," as he was called, was a prolific painter, calligrapher, and poet who also earned notoriety for his dismissal of Zen titles, lineage, and authority, which he viewed as hypocrisy in the monastic community. As represented wonderfully in his poetry, he is also well known for his incredibly permissive attitudes towards alcohol and sex, which he viewed as every bit as sacred as sutras, and just as worthy as potential vehicles for awakening.

101 Four-Year-Olds, Everyone

102 Reflection

Hint: Read this in a mirror.

103 A Place, A Visit, A Word, A Gift

A deep bow of gratitude to Jack Kornfield for inspiring this visualization, which I was introduced to as part of his online master class, The Dynamic Art of Interactive, Guided Meditation, which can be found by visiting his site, jackkornfield.com. I find Jack Kornfield's work, including his online classes, meditations, talks, and interviews, to be tremendously insightful, warm-hearted, transformative, and inspiring, and I recommend them all. A deep bow to you, Jack.

104 Turning Maslow on His Head

Credit to my teacher, The Rt Rev Anthony Stultz, who makes this same point in Free Your Mind: The Four Directions System of Mindfulness. This has proven to be a powerful concept for many people, particularly those who may be without a home, struggling with addiction, incarcerated, etc., and see spiritual transcendence as out of reach. This flipping of the pyramid is intended to challenge this notion.

105 The Water Mirror

This fable is based on the Buddha's teachings on "the five hindrances," which are desire, ill-will (or hatred), sloth (or torpor), worry (or restlessness), and doubt (or despair). Classically, these are described more fully in the Sangarava Sutta, and further in the Avarana Sutta. Additionally, they are referenced in the Satipatthana Sutta, which is an incredibly important text regarding the Buddha's teachings on the foundations of mindfulness. Here, I'd be remiss if I didn't mention and recommend Joseph Goldstein's, Mindfulness: A Practical Guide to Awakening, which is a very thorough and wonderful deep dive into the Sattipatthana Sutta.

106 Note from the Desert

107 The Sun Is Always Rising

108 Reminders